Wild
HORSES

JOHN HAGEE

ISBN: 978-1-951701-43-7

Assembled and Produced for Goose Creek Publishing by
Breakfast for Seven
2150 E. Continental Blvd., Southlake, TX 76092

Printed in the United States of America.

Table of Contents

Receive the Good Plans the Lord has for you.

Out on the open range, a wild stallion is full of energy, passion, and life. He is powerful and submits to no one. If a cowboy rides out onto the prairie and needs to catch a stallion, he must first chase him down, rope him, and rein him in. Once that stallion is back in a corral at the ranch, he must be calmed and broken before he can be ridden and put to work on the range.

Anger, fear, worry, and discipline are each emotions that we all deal with and must all wrestle and tame in our lives. If we are unable to rein in any one of those four emotions, they have the power to destroy us. Any one of them, left unchecked, will only leave destruction and death in their wake.

All of us have emotions that must be corralled if we are to achieve our destiny in life. One of the most difficult aspects of a Christian's life is learning how to control our emotions. Unbridled emotions are a door for Satan to attack your health, mind, relationships, and life.

In this devotional, Pastor Hagee gives clear, Biblical points on how you can overcome the torrent of emotions that buffet against your soul and harness them to further the Kingdom of God. You will find key verses and examples from Scripture that you can use to overcome the attacks of the enemy and keep walking on righteous paths that lead to your destiny and open doors to unlimited success.

We all have emotions. We have all felt anger, worry, or fear at one point or another. The chief issue, however, is to remain in control of your emotions and not let them control you. Uncontrolled, unrestrained, and wild emotions can destroy everything you have built in your life and everything you cherish. However, if you follow Biblical principles to control and rule over them, you can rise to the next level in your life and not let the trials and pains of life derail you.

This devotional was created for you to utilize as a tool to help you understand some of the common emotions we have and gain practical steps to sanctify them and cause them to submit to God. It is a guide that you can use to help you pray, read the Word to renew your mind and conform your heart to the things of God, and receive the good plans the Lord has for you.

Section 1:

A Godly Cause

In Matthew 21, we have a recorded fact that tells us about a time when Jesus Christ, the Son of God, became angry. In colorful detail, Matthew regales us with the account of what happens when the zeal of the Lord breaks forth in righteous indignation. Cut to Jerusalem, and the scene is the Second Temple. However, instead of a house of worship, we find a marketplace:

> Then Jesus went into the temple of God and drove out all those who bought and sold in the temple, and overturned the tables of the money changers and the seats of those who sold doves. And He said to them, "It is written, 'My house shall be called a house of prayer,' but you have made it a 'den of thieves.' " (MATTHEW 21:12–13, NKJV)

In many cases, Jesus (and Christianity as a whole) has been portrayed as a passive, get-along-with-everyone kind of persona, but as we see, that just wasn't the case. Indeed, Jesus loved everyone. Romans 5:8 says, *"But God demonstrates his own love for us in this: While we were still sinners, Christ died for us"* (NIV). He loved the world, but He did not get along with everyone.

In this text, Jesus Christ, the Lamb of God, is angry. He walks into the Second Temple in the center of Jerusalem and goes into a state of rage. Why? Did He sin? Or was His anger righteous and justified? You can be angry and not sin. You can be filled with righteous zeal and indignation and passion and give no cause for sin to overtake you. Jesus showed us how.

Living a righteous life doesn't mean you get along with everyone you meet. One day, Jesus was teaching in a synagogue. But His message was not all about feeling good. He said, *"Either assume the tree to be good as well as its fruit good, or assume the tree to be bad as well as its fruit bad; for the tree is known by its fruit. You offspring of vipers, how can you, being evil, express any good things? For the mouth speaks from that which fills the heart"* (Matthew 12:33–34, NASB). He called the congregation gathered there that day a generation of vipers and hypocrites, snakes and fakes.

It's both a comfort and a challenge to consider that Jesus didn't get along with everybody. It's a comfort because we can't get along with everybody either. It's a challenge because it makes us think about the divine nature of Christ, and we come face-to-face with the fact that God's thoughts and ways are higher than ours.

What is His divine nature, really? When Jesus entered the temple that day, to Him, it was the house of God. The zeal of the Lord consumed Him because He knew it was to be a house of prayer. But instead, it had been converted into an extortionists' bazaar where devout Jews were being robbed in the name of God.

What is the issue that you have made the cause of your life? Does zeal for the house of the Lord consume you? Or have you let the pleasures of life and the desire for other things sway your emotions and seduce you into the trappings of the world?

> You can be filled with righteous zeal and indignation and passion and give no cause for sin to overtake you. Jesus showed us how.

Be Ye Angry, and Sin Not

Have you ever been angry? I mean, really angry? Have you ever been red-faced, eye-popping, foaming at the mouth, fist-waving, foot-stomping angry? It's a type of anger where you're the bull in the ring and all you see is red.

Anger is a powerful emotion, and it is set in the heart of every person. It is divinely planted inside of us and can be used for constructive or destructive purposes. There's something that makes every person uniquely angry. What is it for you?

We often use the phrase "getting mad" to describe our anger. It's a fitting description because, as a general rule, when we lose our temper, we are in a state of insanity. But the fact is that sometimes anger is helpful and necessary. Edmund Burke said, "The only thing necessary for evil to triumph in the world is that good men do nothing."[i] The question then is, "Can one get angry but not sin?" The answer is clear as day.

Ephesians 4:26–27 says: *"Be ye angry, and sin not: let not the sun go down upon your wrath: Neither give place to the devil"* (KJV). Clearly, it is possible to feel anger, as Jesus did that day in the temple courts, do something about it, and not sin in the whole process.

It's all about the cause and reason for your anger in the first place. Was it necessary, or was it misguided? Matthew 5:21–22 says, *"You have heard that it was said to those of old, 'You shall not murder, and whoever murders will be in danger of the judgment.' But I say to you that whoever is angry with his brother without a cause shall be in danger of the judgment. And whoever says to his brother, 'Raca!' shall be in danger of the council. But whoever says, 'You fool!' shall be in danger of hell fire"* (NKJV).

Do you see that phrase "without a cause"? There are times that the cause calls for anger because it is good and right. When we see the scourge of human trafficking, the flood of readily available opioids and drugs, and open rebellion to the Bible, there is just cause for righteous anger that confronts evil, resists the devil, and lifts high a banner unto our God.

Your emotions were divinely given to you by God to be used for good and the advancement of His Kingdom on the earth. They're Heaven's way of mobilizing you for a fight that's worth the doing. They must not be destroyed or given over to the world. They must be controlled and harnessed, put to use, and consecrated to the glory of God and to achieve the purposes of God for your life and the good of others.

We must become passionate about the Word of God. We must become passionate about holiness. We must become passionate about righteousness. We say we want to be like Christ, to become more and more like Him, but how did He respond when He saw injustice and unrighteousness? What did He do in the courts of the temple of Jerusalem? He didn't say, "It's not My problem." Or "Well, I'm not doing it, so I'll just keep minding My business." Jesus, unlike many of us, was consumed with zeal for the Lord, and it drove Him to action.

> Your emotions were divinely given to you by God to be used for good and the advancement of His Kingdom on the earth.

Christ Our Example

Picture the scene. Imagine a devout Jewish man from Galilee. He has looked over his flock and carefully selected the best lamb he has. He then prepares his bag, makes his plans, and begins to travel to Jerusalem with his animal sacrifice. Now the distance from Galilee to Jerusalem is about 80 miles, so to travel by foot while driving his animal, it takes him three or four days to make the one-way journey.

Finally, he arrives in the city. He and his animal squeeze through Jaffa Gate, and immediately he finds himself in an unfamiliar environment while buskers loudly call out to him to come into their shops. He winds through the narrow maze of streets in the walled city and makes his way to the temple. But now he finds himself standing in a long and pushy crowd of people surrounded by rows and rows of lambs, bulls, turtledoves, and pigeons.

The outer court of the temple had become a dirty, smelly, noisy marketplace. The deafening den of sellers hocking their wares, the bleating of sheep, the cackling of caged birds, the bargaining of money changers, and the bellowing of the oxen were drowning out the voices of the religious racketeers, extorting the people from one currency to another. As they say in Hebrew, the whole thing was a "balagan" (a big mess)!

And when the devout traveler finally gets to the front of the crowd, he offers his animal to the high priest for inspection. But the high priest barely looks at the lamb, waves his hand, and quickly dismisses the animal saying, "There is a blemish. Unclean."

So what must the devout worshipper do? He has no choice but to give up his animal and put it in a pen while another priest pulls out another one and sells it to him for an exorbitant price. This new lamb he must now buy with what is left of his money and offer to the high priest as his offering. Unsurprisingly, this "new" lamb is immediately accepted. And what happened to the lamb he brought all the way from Galilee? It is sold to a different pilgrim! But the ploy didn't stop with the priests. The moneychangers were involved as well, looking to get their cut. They were changing currencies and cheating on the change. And the cycle of extortion continues.

The people of God were being extorted, and Jesus was angry. And justifiably so. He made a whip of twisted cords, His eyes became a blazing inferno, and He invaded the court, sweeping money bags to the floor and knocking tables to the ground. He scattered the coins and chased out the moneychangers. One and then another. The avenger of God stormed through the swirl, driving out the cattle and releasing the doves, the sheep, and the goats. In the madness of the marketplace, Jesus of Nazareth stormed. Jesus, a Jewish Rabbi, Jesus, the God of love and mercy, not to worship but to fight against the false values that had been brought in by religion, tradition, and greed.

And what was Jesus' response? He said, *"It is written, 'My house shall be called a house of prayer,' but you have made it a 'den of thieves'"* (Matthew 21:13, NKJV).

> Jesus, the Son of God, cleaned house that day. He showed us that day, like a resounding trumpet call, that when the cause is righteous, anger is love's clearest voice.

What Moses
Lost

Here is a sobering bit of wisdom for you today. If you let anger go unchecked in your heart, eventually it will kill you. Uncontrolled anger will destroy your life because unrighteous anger is sin. Romans 6:23 tells us that *"the wages of sin is death"* (NIV). It is a Biblical fact then that if you let anger brood in your heart like a chicken in its nest, unwilling to move and consumed with itself, it will breed death in your life.

Look at the Bible's parade of men who destroyed their lives because of uncontrolled anger. Consider Moses. Though he spoke with God face-to-face, as one speaks to a friend (Exodus 33:11), because of anger, he would never enter the Promised Land of Israel. Anger kept him from experiencing the one thing he had been dreaming about for 40 years. It kept him from his greatest heart's desire!

Moses' uncontrolled anger first appeared when he murdered an Egyptian. And because of that outburst, Moses had to leave his life in the palace and spend 40 years on the backside of a desert. The next time Moses lost his cool was when he saw the golden calf that the people had constructed at the foot of Mount Sinai. He had just led them out of bondage in Egypt, and they had already turned away to idols. Moses smashed the tablets on the ground and had to go back up the mountain again.

The greatest error of Moses' life, however, came at Kadesh. In Numbers 20, there was no water for the people to drink. Moses and Aaron asked God what to do about the problem, and God said, *"Take the staff; and you and your brother Aaron assemble the congregation and speak to the rock before their eyes, that it shall yield its water. So you shall bring water for them out of the rock, and have the congregation and their livestock drink."* (v. 8, NASB).

But Moses disobeyed what God had said. They indeed gathered the people, but said, *"Listen now, you rebels; shall we bring water for you out of this rock?"* (v. 10). Then Moses struck the rock twice, and water came out abundantly. Had Moses spoken to the rock, the people would have said that God had done the miracle and received the glory. But Moses said, *"Shall we bring water for you out of this rock?"* and hit the rock in anger. Because of that, Moses would die in the wilderness and never enter the Promised Land.

This is a serious lesson for you and me. Moses was a man who walked with God in a way most people never will, but even still, because of anger that led to sin, he died just as Romans 6:23 warns. Moses became so frustrated with the conduct of other people that it affected his relationship with God. The result is that it killed his dream.

What will be your story? Will you allow anger to control your life, or will you bridle it and make it submit to God? The stakes are indeed high. The choices you make or don't make today impact not only your future but also the lives of those around you. If you have outbursts of anger that streak into your life like lightning in a night storm, it is time to run with all your might into the arms of God. And there, under the shadow of the Almighty, find rest for your soul.

> The choices you make or don't make today impact not only your future but also the lives of those around you.

The Cost of Anger
Uncontrolled

Anger by itself is not a sinful emotion. There are no bad emotions, for they are all God-given. Emotions are simply what they are, and as such, they can be used for righteous or evil purposes. When a baby is born, he or she is new to the world and responds to the world with raw emotions. If there is something wrong, they cry. The crying of a baby is not good or bad; it is the baby's natural response.

But as we grow up, we learn to control our emotions. We learn to harness our anger and interact with the world as we should. Uncontrolled anger, however, is sin. If you're a grown man and you claim you follow Jesus as your Lord, you can't go around wrapping your golf clubs around a tree anytime a shot splices off into the woods. It's not the golf club's fault. It is anger unabated in the heart.

It's not a sin to be angry, but it is a sin to give way to anger. When red-hot emotions are knocking down your door, if they are not of the Lord, do not let them lead you to sin and do not let them control you. Uncontrolled anger will rob you of your life. It has the capacity to destroy the relationships of those closest to you because, when you explode, the fragments of your hot head will devastate those around you. Sin that is not dealt with as what it is — open rebellion to God — leads down only one path. Every time and without fail, the path of sin leads only to destruction, for the wages of sin is death.

Uncontrolled anger can release chemical poisons into your body that cause disease and ailment. Angry people are more prone to heart attacks, cancer, ulcers, and strokes. When you let yourself live in a state of uncontrolled rage, you are not just committing sin; you are slowly destroying your body.

Don't let your dreams be derailed by uncontrolled anger or your marriage destroyed by hateful words. Don't damage your relationships with your children or burn bridges with your friends. If anger has a hold on you, go to the Lord. His Word, His ways, and His presence can transform you into a new creation.

The Bible is filled with accounts of those who let anger get the better of them. In Genesis 4, Cain's uncontrolled anger drove him to murder his brother in cold blood. Why? Because he was angry that God accepted Abel's sacrifice. Be careful not to become angry over God's blessings in the lives of other people.

Or consider the elder brother of the Prodigal Son. When the younger brother finally returned home and the father killed the fattened calf in celebration, the elder brother would not come into the house. He was more angry with his father's mercy than with his relationship with his brother. He couldn't handle seeing someone else forgiven and restored.

There will always be a cost to everything you do and everything you say. For your good or at your expense. What will the cost of uncontrolled anger be in your life? Galatians 6:7 says, *"Whatever one sows, that will he also reap"* (ESV). Put a bridle on anger by coming to the throne of grace in repentance. If there is sin, confess it and move on. Ask the Lord to fill you with the fruit of the Spirit and go out as one who has laid their burden down.

> If anger has a hold on you, go to the Lord. His Word, His ways, and His presence can transform you into a new creation.

What Are You Mad At?

We can get mad about so many things. Some of the things we get angry about are justifiable. Others, not so much. If someone isn't driving fast enough in front of you on the highway and you blow your top because you want them to go 20 miles over the speed limit like you are, you might have an anger problem.

But not all anger is bad. What made Jesus angry? One day, He was teaching in the temple in Jerusalem. He was teaching the people about the Kingdom of God, and the Pharisees wanted to have a discussion about who Abraham's descendants were because they wanted to make much of themselves and their names. "Abraham is our father," they said, but Jesus gave them an answer they wouldn't forget:

Jesus said to them, "If God were your Father, you would love me, for I came from God and I am here. I came not of my own accord, but he sent me. Why do you not understand what I say? It is because you cannot bear to hear my word. You are of your father the devil, and your will is to do your father's desires" (John 8:42–44, ESV). It was a rather politically incorrect statement at the time to say that their father was the devil, but Jesus was not afraid to tell them who they really were.

It's not worth your time to sweat the small stuff or get involved in fruitless conversations with people who are only interested in pushing their agenda. As a blood-bought believer, you have more important things to do and eternal endeavors to set your hand toward.

We would do well to heed Paul's exhortation to the church in Ephesus: *"Finally, be strong in the Lord and in the strength of his might. Put on the whole armor of God, that you may be able to stand against the schemes of the devil. For we do not wrestle against flesh and blood, but against the rulers, against the authorities, against the cosmic powers over this present darkness, against the spiritual forces of evil in the heavenly places. Therefore take up the whole armor of God, that you may be able to withstand in the evil day, and having done all, to stand firm"* (Ephesians 6:10–13, ESV).

If you're going to get mad about something, get hopping mad about the advance of the forces of evil across the nations of the earth and the hearts of men. You have your marching orders here in these verses. Paul's appeal was for the church to engage the enemy where he stands. To put on armor for a fight and take back what the enemy has stolen, killed, and destroyed. With the Lord on your side, you can push back the darkness and watch the enemy be scattered.

You must learn to harness the tornado of anger that has buffeted your soul and brought destruction to your life. If you want to accomplish the purposes of God in your life, you must resist the enemy, and he will flee from you (James 4:7). If you stand in the strength of the Lord, you will overcome.

Submit yourself then wholly to God. Commit your heart, soul, mind, and body unto Him. And when you do, the Lord will help you conquer every emotion in your life that keeps you from reaching your divine po-tential. And in His grace, may He give you the desires of your heart and set you on your high heights (Habakkuk 3:19).

> If you stand in the strength of the Lord, you will overcome.

Anger Can Be Constructive

If the cause is godly, there are times that anger is called for. There are situations in which anger is good. The question in any given scenario is, "What is the motivation of that anger?" It can be a powerful force when harnessed correctly and constructively and spiritually directed. It was a righteous moment that is heralded in the halls of Heaven to this day when Jesus, with whip in hand, stood in the gap in holy advocation for the devout Jews who had come to Jerusalem to worship.

Jesus stood against evil and made it bow before Him. He is the *"Son of God, who has eyes like a flame of fire"* (Revelation 2:18, NKJV). He made evil cower before Him and took by force the keys of Hades and Death. He invaded the stronghold of the grave and returned victorious.

Anger can be constructive when it is born out of righteous purposes. All around us, false values are presented across our nation and in the house of God. And I believe it enrages our loving, compassionate God today, just as it did 2,000 years ago. What will our response be? There is a time to get up and allow righteous anger to motivate you to take divine action against false values.

America has become saturated with *"those who call evil good and good evil, who put darkness for light and light for darkness"* (Isaiah 5:20, NIV). We have become a nation where paganism, hedonism, and ungodliness are celebrated. We are seeing darkness substituted for light and the sweet exchanged for the bitter. Right now, before our eyes, in these United States, judges and lawmakers are abandoning morality and sanity and codifying evil.

This is the agenda of the radical left in America. To push God out of every corner of society that they possibly can. Their aim is to erase the name of Jesus and give way to the god of man. Their intention is to remove anyone who will not bow to their form of lifestyle. And morality is mocked while perversion is paraded in the streets.

The fruit of this is nothing short of lawlessness. We've become a society of drive-by shootings, drugs, divorce, delinquency, and death. We have become a nation that has flung wide the gates to paganism and handed our homes over to the enemy. But there is an answer, and the answer is for the church to bear the words of King David who said, *"Ye that love the LORD, hate evil"* (Psalm 97:10, KJV).

When we commit to hating evil and loving the Lord, we draw a line in the sand and begin to retake lost territory. We must not sit back and watch the enemy devour our children, destroy our marriages, devastate our finances, and demolish our health without so much as raising a word of protest.

The tragedy of our day is that the situation is desperate, but the church is not. We must not merely talk of holiness and righteousness and godliness, but rise up, lift high the standard of the Gospel, and charge the gates of Hell.

When we commit to hating evil and loving the Lord, we draw a line in the sand and begin to retake lost territory.

God Gets
Angry

One day, Jesus was teaching in a synagogue on the Sabbath. In the congregation that day was a man with a withered hand. The religious leaders closely watched Jesus. What would He do? Would He "work" and therefore break the Sabbath by healing the man that they might accuse Him? They watched Him intently.

But Jesus told the crippled man to step forward and said, *"Is it lawful on the Sabbath to do good or to do evil, to save life or to kill?" But they kept silent. And when He had looked around at them with anger, being grieved by the hardness of their hearts, He said to the man, "Stretch out your hand." And he stretched it out, and his hand was restored as whole as the other* (Mark 3:4–5, NKJV).

Jesus was not only grieved by the hardness of their hearts, He was also angry about it. The pharisees were more concerned with keeping the requirements of how they interpreted the law — that they placed religion over people. In their minds, nothing spiritual should happen on the Sabbath, not even if it meant healing someone in pain.

But Jesus doesn't operate that way. He had also said, *"The Sabbath was made for man, and not man for* the Sabbath" (Mark 2:27, NKJV). He is the Great Physician. He is the binder of the brokenhearted. He is Jehovah Rophe. If you're sick, He can heal you today or any other day. He can take the disease, the sickness, whatever it is, and He can make you whole.

When God gets angry, it's often about standing up for righteousness, justice, and love. It's when His people have gone astray and chased after other gods — doing things that hurt themselves and others as well. But the Bible says that God is a jealous God. He is jealous for your heart, and He is jealous for your love.

God is not out of touch with your life. He is near, and He is active in every area of your life. Exodus 34:14 says, *"Do not worship any other god, for the LORD, whose name is Jealous, is a jealous God"* (NIV). If you would seek to avoid the jealousy of God, take a leaf from the book of what the Israelites learned and do all you can to neither serve any other god nor let idolatry into your life.

He is Holy, High and Lifted Up, and seated in the Heavens. With Him, there is no place for blatant sin or open rebellion. If God judged Sodom and Gomorrah for pride, rebellion, and the lust of the flesh that seared their minds with depravity, He will judge America and the nations of the world as well.

Salvation is found in Christ and Christ alone. John 3:36 says, *"He who believes in the Son has everlasting life; and he who does not believe the Son shall not see life, but the wrath of God abides on him"* (NKJV). Only through Jesus does man find the path of life. Only in Christ doth the wrath of God subside.

Wholehearted devotion to God is what will bring the greatest joy to your life. Jesus said, *"Seek first the kingdom of God and his righteousness, and all these things will be added to you"* (Matthew 6:33, ESV). If you are looking for respite from wrath and would seek the good plans that God has for your life, you will find it when you seek Him above all else.

> The Bible says that God is a jealous God. He is jealous for your heart, and He is jealous for your love.

When It's Right
to Be Angry

There are some things worth getting angry about. There are some injustices in the world that are so grievous that to stand by passively and do nothing is simply wrong. Ecclesiastes 3:1 says, *"There is a time for everything, and a season for every activity under the heavens"* (NIV). In verse 8, it tells us there is even a time for peace and for war. Sometimes, anger is right.

The motto of the United States Army Special Forces is the Latin phrase, *"De oppresso liber."* Translated, it means "to free the oppressed." Ingrained in the training of the United States Armed Forces is not only to "defend the Constitution of the United States against all enemies, foreign and domestic"[ii] but also to free the oppressed.

James 2 asks us what good it is for someone to claim they have faith but no deeds to back up their words. If someone is without clothes or food, it means nothing to say to them, *"Go in peace; keep warm and well fed"* (v. 16), but not provide for their needs. Faith, he says, *"not accompanied by action, is dead"* (v. 17, NIV).

How can we love people and stand by while they are wounded or exploited? Righteous indignation that leads to action is not only the right thing to do but can also lead to the saving of many lives. Florence Nightingale was born into a wealthy British family in 1820. She was expected to live the life of a socialite, but from a young age, she felt the divine call on her life was in the field of nursing.

At the time, British field hospitals were horribly unsanitary. More soldiers were dying from infection at the hospitals than from wounds in battle. When Florence Nightingale arrived at the British hospital in Constantinople during the Crimean War, she was shocked by the conditions and sprang into action to improve them. Her work and her 830-page report, *"Notes on Matters Affecting the Health, Efficiency and Hospital Administration of the British Army,"* would lead to a complete overhaul of not only the British hospital administration of that day but eventually lead to reform around the world. Today, she is widely regarded as the pioneer of modern-day nursing. And it all started because a woman with a call of God on her life would not give up.[iii]

What will it be for you? What is it that makes you so angry you are compelled to action? The very thing that makes you angry could very well be the thing that God has given you for your work in the world. The hour is late. The time for action is now. We must no longer be content to live as casual Christians, dabbling in everything but committed to nothing. It is time to become angry enough to confess that we have been seduced by the world, the flesh, and the devil — that we have compromised our convictions for ease and our vows for the pleasures of the world.

It is time to say, "Enough is enough." It is time to say, "Not on my watch." It is time to be more consumed with zeal for the Lord than the opinions of man. Who will rise up? Who will answer the call? Who will be angry enough with righteous indignation to storm the gates of darkness in the authority of the name of Jesus Christ? Who will challenge the forces of evil and declare, "The righteous will not bow!"

The very thing that makes you angry could very well be the thing that God has given you for your work in the world.

When It's Wrong to Be Angry

Anger is not a fruit of the spirit. And there are times when it is wrong to be angry. Misguided or misdirected anger does not fit in the growing life of a believer and one who has pledged loyalty to Jesus Christ as Lord. Indeed, in the Sermon on the Mount, Jesus gave us clear direction regarding the subject of anger, saying: *"You have heard that it was said, 'You shall love your neighbor and hate your enemy.' But I say to you, love your enemies, bless those who curse you, do good to those who hate you, and pray for those who spitefully use you and persecute you, that you may be sons of your Father in heaven"* (Matthew 5:43–45, NKJV).

When Jesus stepped on the scene, He was more concerned that we love our enemies than we avenge ourselves upon them. His was a call to radical love, even in the face of persecution. Anger then, held within the heart that does not have a cause, is misguided and out of place.

It's wrong to be angry when we are so because other people are being treated better than we are. It's the elder brother syndrome from the story of the prodigal son. When we are bitter, resentful, and speaking hateful things about other people, we make no room for love. Philippians 2:3 says it this way: *"Do nothing from self-ishness or empty conceit, but with humility consider one another as more important than yourselves"* (NASB).

A wrathful person in the home, in the church, in the nation, in marriage, on the job, or on any team is poison in the pot. Proverbs 15:18 says, *"A wrathful man stirreth up strife: but he that is slow to anger appeaseth strife"* (KJV). If there is someone in your life who is habitually blowing their top when you're around them, remember that "he who is slow to anger calms dispute."

Solomon is considered the wisest man who ever lived after God indued him with wisdom (1 Kings 3:12). What did he say about living with someone who was angry? The man who had 700 wives said, *"Better to dwell in the wilderness, than with a contentious and angry woman"* (Proverbs 21:19, NKJV). And what did his wives do? They *"turned his heart af-ter other gods; and his heart was not loyal to the LORD his God"* (1 Kings 11:4, NKJV). There is a place for anger, and there is a place for peace. Solomon lived with hundreds of wives, and as one who had the wisest heart on earth, he said that it was better to be alone than to live with someone who was angry.

As believers, we're called to overlook offense and make way for love and reconciliation. Proverbs 19:11 says, *"The discretion of a man makes him slow to anger, and his glo-ry is to overlook a transgression"* (NKJV). What does that mean? It means you don't have to fixate on everything that happens to you. That it is better to forgive and move on than to hold someone's feet to the fire because of something they did that crossed you 20 years ago.

There is a time and a place for everything under the sun. And that means there is a right time for anger and a wrong time for anger. Does your cause for anger line up with the Word of God? If so, pursue it and do so wholeheartedly. If not, overlook the transgression and keep moving forward.

> As believers, we're called to overlook offense and make way for love and reconciliation.

How to Control Your Anger

When it comes to controlling anger, you have the greatest example known to man. There is no greater example than Jesus, the Christ and Son of God. He lived a perfect life, never sinning once, but He was no pushover when it came to matters of injustice, love, or zeal for God.

On behalf of others, He was the Lion. When it came to Himself, He became obedient to death, even the death on the Cross. And on that day, on Golgotha's hill, He said, *"Father, forgive them; for they know not what they do"* (Luke 23:34, KJV). He was, is, and will be the answer to any anger that has taken up residence in your heart.

Look to God constantly. In Him, you may be conformed to the image of His Son. In Him, you will find what it means to live a life that is marked by Heaven on earth. Sanctification is a continual recalibration of the heart. It is a constant crucifying of the flesh. It is a heart that knows that the answer to overcoming anger is found in the One who formed you and knit you together in your mother's womb.

Jesus is the answer to your life, and in Him you will find all that you need. He is our model and standard. And what did He do? He cleansed the temple as the avenger of God, filled with zeal for the house of the Lord. And yet, when He was personally attacked, He did not retaliate. In the garden of Gethsemane on the Mount of Olives, He was betrayed, arrested, and led away as a prisoner. He would be beaten, ridiculed, and mocked with a crown of thorns on His head and a robe on His back. When accusations railed against Him, He answered not a word (Matthew 27:14).

Instead, He fulfilled Isaiah's prophetic word concerning Him: *"He was oppressed and He was afflicted, yet He opened not His mouth; He was led as a lamb to the slaughter, and as a sheep before its shearers is silent, so He opened not His mouth"* (Isaiah 53:7, NKJV). Though led like a lamb, He opened not His mouth. That's control. Without a word, He stood before Pilate and the mobs who were screaming for His blood.

Long suffering is the opposite of anger. But you cannot do it in your own strength. It is only possible when we walk in the Spirit. It is a daily process of dying to yourself and drinking the living water of the Word of God. To overlook transgression is to walk by faith in the Spirit. Galatians 5:22–23 says, *"The fruit of the Spirit is love, joy, peace, patience, kindness, goodness, faithfulness, gentleness, self-control; against such things there is no law"* (ESV). Since we live by the Spirit, let us keep in step with the Spirit.

How do we control our anger? By becoming Spirit-filled. The answer to overcoming anger is not found through worldly self-help books or by looking for answers within. The power to overcome anger is only found when you submit to the Lord and Savior of your soul, Jesus Christ. Only in Him and through the power of the Holy Spirit, will you be able to control the wild horse of anger and live a life filled with the fruit of the Spirit.

Jesus is the answer to your life, and in Him you will find all that you need. He is our model and standard.

Avoid Angry People

In life, you will not be able to completely avoid angry people. However, you can make the decision to not let new ones into your life. And if it can't be avoided at all — perhaps someone close to you is given to anger — you still have the capability to set boundaries in your relationship with them.

The Bible is clear on the subject of avoiding angry people, and it is for your good. Proverbs 22:24–25 says, *"Make no friendship with an angry man, and with a furious man do not go, lest you learn his ways and set a snare for your soul"* (NKJV). You see, anger is contagious. Spend enough time with someone, and eventually you begin to become like them. The underlying issue with anger is that you not only learn the ways of the angry man, but that anger itself lays a "snare for your soul."

Is your anger out of control? Seek the Lord while He may be found. Proverbs 16:32 says, *"He that is slow to anger is better than the mighty; and he that ruleth his spirit than he that taketh a city"* (KJV). A man who can control his emotions is greater than one who gives into them. It is the disciplined man who is more righteous than the one who is tossed back and forth by every wish or whim.

Ruling your spirit and disciplining your soul will take you far. Sometimes, it's the loudest voices who you need to be concerned about the least. Not the man who's running his mouth the noisiest, but the man sitting over in the corner with the cold, clear eyes, looking through you. That's the guy that's going to stay with you day after day, month after month. The English poet John Dryden, in his poem *Absalom and Achitophel*, wrote "beware of the fury of a patient man."[iv] Enduring patience is stronger than impulsive wrath.

How do you react when things don't go your way? Do you constantly bring up the past to others or in your own mind? Do you brood over yesterday and things that can't be changed? Offense in relationships happens every day and there is always something you could choose to get upset about. But Peter wrote that it is better to let love cover over sin when he said, *"Above all, love each other deeply, because love covers over a multitude of sins"* (1 Peter 4:8, NIV).

I have learned that it is better to let things go rather than hold on to them. That it is better both for our own selves and our relationships in life to learn to find reasons to laugh. Nehemiah 8:10 says, *"The joy of the LORD is your strength"* (NKJV). Laughter can save you from days of pain. When you laugh, your body releases physiological benefits that can bring healing to your body.[v] Truly, the fruit of anger leads to destruction, but a *"happy heart makes the face cheerful"* (Proverbs 15:13, NIV).

If you want a happy marriage or a long-lasting friendship, you must learn to overlook other people's mistakes, faults, or offenses against you. Conflict in relationships is normal. How you respond when conflict arises however, makes all the difference. When there's no real injury involved, don't live with a chip on your shoulder. Let love cover a multitude of sin.

> The underlying issue with anger is that you not only learn the ways of the angry man, but that anger itself lays a "snare for your soul."

Section 2:

Anxious for Nothing

We all have them. "Wild horse" emotions that, if unbridled, can run roughshod through our souls, lives, and relationships. They can even destroy us. Yet these same wild horse emotions, if brought under control, can carry us to new levels of success. Yes, emotions are powerful. They can fill our minds and shape our thoughts. They can energize or deflate. Propel or paralyze. That's why it is absolutely vital for the believer not to be controlled by emotions.

You may be one who is given over to worry. It may run in your family. If so, it is possible that one of the first things you learned how to do as a kid was worry. Maybe your earliest memories of your parents are seeing them worry and fret around the house. Now you have a Ph.D. in worry. You're a professional worrier, and you came by it honestly.

Do you worry more than you should? Worry is no respecter of persons and is not relegated to one class. It is a common denominator. The rich worry. The poor worry. The intelligent and illiterate worry. Both the young and the old do as well. Some people even worry that they don't worry enough!

God is a God who knows us well. He is well versed in the human condition. Psalm 139 tells us that He formed our inward parts and covered us in our mother's womb. He calls us fearfully and wonderfully made, and all the days ordained for us were written in His book. He knows where we came from, what we're doing, and the inner workings of our hearts.

But what does the Bible say about worry, and what is God's exhortation to us? Philippians 4:6–7 says, *"Be anxious for nothing, but in everything by prayer and supplication, with thanksgiving, let your requests be known to God; and the peace of God, which surpasses all understanding, will guard your hearts and minds through Christ Jesus"* (NKJV).

Those two verses can radically change your life for the better. You see, worry is like a rocking chair. It will give you something to do but it won't get you anywhere. In fact, worry not only brings stagnation to your life, it can actually cause you to slip backwards — pushing you farther away from where you hope to be.

I want you to focus on those four words — be anxious for nothing — because they will help your marriage, your health, your future, and your soul.

For the child of God, peace is your portion. For the blood-bought and redeemed son or daughter, worry has no place in your life. It doesn't fit. It's not who you are. Your citizenship is in Heaven, and no one is pacing back and forth on those streets of gold worrying about all the things God has already taken care of.

If you want to find one of the surest and most clear paths to mental peace and, therefore, peace that over-shadows your life, you would do well to often quote the words of that verse: Be anxious for nothing. Those are words that you need to internalize. They need to be written on your soul. Write them on a card, tape them to your refrigerator, say them out loud throughout the day. If you can fully absorb those four words, it will change your life and even change your family tree.

> For the child of God, peace is your portion. For the blood-bought and redeemed son or daughter, worry has no place in your life.

God Is on His Throne

Psalm 24:1–2 says, *"The earth is the Lord's, and the fulness thereof; the world, and they that dwell therein. For he hath founded it upon the seas, and established it upon the floods"* (KJV). David clearly had a high view of God when he wrote that psalm. He knew that he knew that he knew that nothing is impossible for the Most High King of Heaven and earth. For you and me, that means no matter the problem, no matter the obstacle, no matter the mountain, all must bow before the awesome power of Jehovah on His throne.

When you focus on your problem, you aren't focusing on God's promises, provision, and power. There was a good reason why Psalm 121:1–2 says, *"I will lift up my eyes to the hills — from whence comes my help? My help comes from the Lord, who made heaven and earth"* (NKJV). It's time to lift your eyes from the problem and look toward Heaven. It's time to get a higher view of God and a lower view of the problems, issues, and worries of the earth.

The earth is the Lord's. God is on His throne. He made Heaven and earth, and nothing is impossible for Him. When you place your worries against the backdrop of the eternal promises of Scripture, their power begins to fade like the setting sun.

What then do we worry about? The answer is all too often, "everything." We worry about our health, about the future, and about our financial ability. We worry about politics, our society's declining morals, and the economy. We worry about family and relationships. We worry because it's easy to do and we're good at it. Yet what we need to get good at is remembering the promises of God.

When Paul said, *"Be anxious for nothing,"* he meant be anxious for nothing. Nothing means nothing. Philippians 4:6 is one of my all-time favorite verses. I have found it a comforting pillow upon which to rest my head when I was weary beyond words. I have found it a strong staff upon which to lean when my feet were in slippery places. I have found it to be a fortress in the day of battle. In nothing, be anxious. How reassuring, how full of comfort. It is as tender as a mother's nurture. It is stronger than the everlasting hills. It is a truth that endures throughout the ages.

If you remember that God is on His throne, you begin to find that it is easier to be anxious for nothing. You begin to see that because of Him, everything's going to be all right. You don't need to worry about your health because Jesus Christ is still the Great Physician. You don't need to worry about your finances because your Heavenly Father is Jehovah Jireh.

Lift up your eyes from your problems today and set them on the King of Glory. Lift up every petition to His throne through prayer and supplication, giving thanks to God. He is Lord of All, and He is the Good

Shepherd of your soul. In Him, you will find the peace of God that passes all understanding and find your heart and soul guarded by His precious promises.

> If you remember that God is on His throne, you begin to find that it is easier to be anxious for nothing.

Jehovah Jireh

When Abraham and Isaac went into the land of Moriah and climbed the mountain that the Lord showed him, Abraham believed he was climbing up that mountain to sacrifice his son. Abraham took every step, believing that Isaac was to be the sacrifice. But an incredible thing happened that day, and the Lord showed up in a way that Abraham could never have believed. At the last minute, an angel told him to stay his hand and instead take the ram that was caught by its horns in a nearby thicket.

On that day, Abraham learned something new about God. He learned, and it was recorded for us in the Bible, that God is a God who sees, provides, and makes a way for us where there is no way. Genesis 22:14 says, *"And Abraham called the name of that place Jehovah Jireh: as it is said to this day, in the mount of the Lord it shall be seen"* (KJV).

Abraham had much to think about as he hiked that mountain with his beloved son of promise. He could have let all sorts of thoughts dance through his mind. "Did I really hear God?" "What if God doesn't raise him up from the dead?" "Am I being overly zealous in my obedience?" But hoping against hope, he kept going. By faith, Abraham determined within himself to be obedient to God, even to offer up Isaac. He knew that God had said, *"In Isaac your seed shall be called,"* but he concluded that God was able to raise him up, even from the dead. (Hebrews 11:17–19, NKJV).

You must remember who you are in Christ and Whose you are based on the Word of God. Don't worry about insecurity, about lack, or what may or may not come to pass. It's not your part to worry. It's your part to take God at His Word. To believe Him.

Who are you, really? As Paul said, you are Christ's ambassador (2 Corinthians 5:20). You are a son or a daughter of the King. You have been redeemed, set free, and justified. And today, right now, *"greater is he that is in you, than he that is in the world"* (1 John 4:4, KJV). You are a chosen people and a royal priesthood not because of what you've done for God but because of what Jesus has already done for you (1 Peter 2:9).

The Lord is Jehovah Jireh, and you belong to Him. Since you are now under His care, you must take heed not to let worry enter your thoughts. We need to be warned about worry because worry is sin. It is faith in fear, instead of faith in God. When you worry, you're saying in effect, "I don't believe God can do what He said He can do." Today, focus again on who God is.

We serve a God who has never failed and who cannot fail. He is always faithful, and He cannot be anything other than who He is. He never changes. Hebrews 13:8 says, *"Jesus Christ is the same yesterday and today and forever"* (NIV). If He provided for His people in the wilderness, if He fed the 5,000, if He provided for the widow at Zarephath, He will provide for you.

You are a chosen people and a royal priesthood not because of what you've done for God but because of what Jesus has already done for you (1 Peter 2:9).

A Shot of
Penicillin

Penicillin is perhaps the most widely used antibiotic agent in the world. It was first discovered in 1928 by the Scottish bacteriologist Alexander Fleming. Later, in the 1930s, an Australian pathologist and a British biochemist studied how to isolate and purify it. By 1941, an injectable form was produced, and has now saved the lives of countless people.[vi]

Did you know there is a Bible penicillin shot for worry? There is something you can do right now that will combat the fear and worry that is plaguing your heart and clouding your mind. It is not difficult or lofty, but rather something that even a child could do: the supreme penicillin shot for worry is faith in God.

Having faith in God is not reserved for the monk in the monastery, the tenured seminary professor, or the chaplain slugging it out on a distant battlefield. Having faith in God is not something you have to go on a pilgrimage to obtain, something you buy by putting coins in a coffer or doing penance on your knees.

Faith in God is something that is attainable for anyone. Jesus said, *"Truly I tell you, unless you change and become like little children, you will never enter the king-dom of heaven"* (Matthew 18:3, NIV). It is simply to believe. A heavy burden is not laid upon you. Take your worry and place it before the throne of God today. All that is required of you is to believe on the Lord Jesus and leave every care at your Heavenly Father's feet.

King David wrote, *"Cast your burden on the LORD, and He shall sustain you; He shall never permit the righteous to be moved"* (Psalm 55:22, NKJV). Can you cast your burden down today? Will you let it go? Will you take the penicillin of the Word of God and infuse it into every worry? Pitted against the Word of God, worry will fall every time.

People who carry a Bible that's falling apart have a life that's not. How many verses of Scripture have you memorized? How much of the Word of God do you allow to roll over and over in your mind like waves against the shore? With every crashing break, with each point break, worries and fears crumble like the shifting sand that they are.

Who is God, and what has He said about Himself? *"God is our refuge and strength, a very present help in trouble"* (Psalm 46:1, ESV). Therefore, though the earth give way, though the storms come, though the mountains be shaken, as for us, we will not fear.

Here's the secret: Just start. Even if you don't feel like it, even if you don't see it, even if the mountain of worry is bearing down on you like a falling avalanche, raise your voice and give the Lord praise. Just start lifting your eyes and hands and the hope of your heart to Heaven. Just start praying. Just get the ship out of the harbor and watch with wonder as the Lord directs the sails.

Take your worry and place it before the throne of God today.

Whom Shall I Fear?

You can learn to get rid of the thing you are afraid of or worried about. It's true! Just because a certain worry has hounded you for days, months, or even years doesn't mean it has permission to stay with you for the rest of your life.

At Calvary, Jesus conquered all. The One who humbled Himself and became obedient unto death, even the death of the Cross, is the One who took the keys of Hades and made death and the grave bow before Him. And now He is highly exalted and has the name which is above every other name (Philippians 2:9). Fear must fall. Worry must bow.

As for you, whom or what on earth is left for you to fear? Psalm 27:1 says, *"The LORD is my light and my salvation — whom shall I fear? The LORD is the strong-hold of my life — of whom shall I be afraid?"* (NIV). Listen closely to the words of David, for you have the Lord on your side. With Him, you have all you need. He is your light, He is your salvation, He is your stronghold.

Though the trials of life may come, and though the tribulations of the day may buffet your soul, you are not alone. For the believer, the Lord is always by your side, and you have peace with God. Romans 5:1 says, *"There-fore, since we have been justified by faith, we have peace with God through our Lord Jesus Christ"* (NIV). And if you have peace with God, then you have peace indeed.

Don't worry about your past failure. Give no thought to your past sins, shortcomings, or mistakes. Why? Because God's grace is greater than all your sin. Yes, we have all sinned, but the story doesn't end there. The Cross stands at the crux of history, proclaiming forevermore that Jesus has indeed accomplished all that was necessary to make the way for us to come to God. As the hymn written in 1865 reminds us: *"Jesus paid it all, all to Him I owe; sin had left a crimson stain, He washed it white as snow."* [vii]

There's nothing like walking down the road of life — through all the flak you're going to face — knowing that the peace of God that surpasses all understanding will ever guard your heart and mind. Therefore, it makes no difference what may come today or tomorrow because, if you have pledged your allegiance to the Lamb of God for the salvation of your soul, then in the end, it's going to be all right.

Remember that the Keeper of your soul reigns for-ever from Heaven above. *"The LORD is your protector; The LORD is your shade on your right hand. The sun will not beat down on you by day, nor the moon by night. The LORD will protect you from all evil; He will keep your soul. The LORD will guard your going out and your coming in from this time and forever"* (Psalm 121:5–8, NASB).

Let worry fall by the wayside, for angels go before you to escort you, and angels go behind you. Demons tremble when you pray in Jesus' name. Nothing is impossible unto you. You are a child of the King. Think like it, talk like it, and act like it. Now nothing can defeat you because you have *"become the righteousness of God"* (2 Corinthians 5:21, NIV), and as for you, your feet are on the Solid Rock.

> The Cross stands at the crux of history, proclaiming forevermore that Jesus has indeed accomplished all that was necessary to make the way for us to come to God.

Psalm 91

If you open your Bible to about the middle, you will find yourself in the neighborhood of a psalm that can alleviate your worries and strengthen your soul. It is packed full of promises, encouragement, and hope. If you read it daily, you would find many worries begin to fade away. It is Psalm 91.

It begins with a call to abide in God: *"Whoever dwells in the shelter of the Most High will rest in the shadow of the Almighty. I will say of the LORD, 'He is my refuge and my fortress, my God, in whom I trust'"* (vv. 1–2, NIV). Herein lays the foundation to peace in life — resting, dwelling, and staying as close to God as you possibly can.

To those who plant themselves close to God, the promises and assurances roll in like an unstoppable storm. *"Surely he will save you from the fowler's snare and from the deadly pestilence. He will cover you with his feathers, and under his wings you will find refuge; his faithfulness will be your shield and rampart. You will not fear the terror of night, nor the arrow that flies by day, nor the pestilence that stalks in the darkness, nor the plague that destroys at midday"* (vv. 3–6, NIV). Surely, He is the One who will save you. Surely, He will cover you and protect you all the days of your life.

Disaster will not overtake you. Tragedy will not be your lot, for: *"A thousand may fall at your side, ten thousand at your right hand, but it will not come near you. You will only observe with your eyes and see the punishment of the wicked"* (vv. 7–8, NIV). Because you have made the Lord your hope, you can claim the goodness of the protection of Heaven.

All that you need is found in God. *"If you say, 'The Lord is my refuge,' and you make the Most High your dwelling, no harm will overtake you, no disaster will come near your tent. For he will command his angels concerning you to guard you in all your ways; they will lift you up in their hands, so that you will not strike your foot against a stone. You will tread on the lion and the cobra; you will trample the great lion and the serpent"* (vv. 9–13, NIV). Angels surround you and keep you from the attacks of the enemy.

And as the psalm comes to a crescendo, hope for the day and unto tomorrow will rise in your soul. *"Because he loves me,"* says the Lord, *"I will rescue him; I will protect him, for he acknowledges my name. He will call on me, and I will answer him; I will be with him in trouble, I will deliver him and honor him. With long life I will satisfy him and show him my salvation"* (vv. 14–16, NIV).

You can call on God, and He will answer you. You are not alone. You have a Shepherd-King who loves you, has promised to be with you, and has a good plan for your life. He is near in trouble, and He is close in tribulation. All that is left for you is to draw near.

The Word of God is living and active. Believe on God's Word. Do not just keep it by your bedside or skim over it in the morning. It is life to your soul, it is breath to your spirit, and it is nourishment to your being. Apply Psalm 91 to your worry like a healing balm for your pain. Overlay the verses against your concerns and fears. Your mind is your own. Fill it today with truth and that which is noble, praiseworthy, and right.

> You have a Shepherd-King who loves you, has promised to be with you, and has a good plan for your life.

Take No Thought

In Matthew 5–7, we have perhaps the greatest sermon ever recorded. The Sermon on the Mount was Jesus' exhortation on how to live, how to interact with our fellow man, and even how to pray. Much wise instruction in life and godliness can be found within these three chapters.

In the sixth chapter, Jesus addresses worry head-on. He does not beat around the bush, and He does not overcomplicate it. Simply, He says: do not worry. We are not to worry about food, clothing, or even our life. *"Therefore I say to you, do not worry about your life, what you will eat or what you will drink; nor about your body, what you will put on. Is not life more than food and the body more than clothing?"* (6:25, NKJV).

We are to take no thought for the cares of this life. That doesn't mean we don't work or tend to our responsibilities. But there is a difference in being diligent with our duty for each day and worrying about the outcomes of things we cannot change. Jesus said, *"Take therefore no thought for the morrow: for the morrow shall take thought for the things of itself. Sufficient unto the day is the evil thereof"* (6:34, KJV).

Our Heavenly Father knows what we need. He knows we need food, clothing, and shelter. He knows we have things that we need in order to live. The difference is whether or not we approach the needs of life as the end-all-be-all or if we keep them in their proper place.

Smack dab in the middle of His message on worry, Jesus spins the topic. While the people sitting on the hills of Galilee were listening to the Master Teacher, He turns the subject on its head and reveals a secret to life in the Kingdom of God.

If we would obtain all that we need, one thing is needed, and that is a life that is tuned to God. Jesus said, *"Seek first the kingdom of God and His righteousness, and all these things shall be added to you"* (6:33, NKJV). There's the secret: "Seek first." That means that before we run after that designer sweater, we seek first the Kingdom of God. Before we order that jalapeño pepper, we seek first the Kingdom of God. Before we do anything at all, we order our lives to place God first and foremost above all things.

That goes for your mind, your thought life, and to what you choose to give your energy and effort. Jesus said, "Take no thought" to the concerns of life. Give no place to worry, for it will only rob your life and leave nothing in its wake.

But if you would have a mind renewed by the Word of God, if you would have a soul that is alive to the things of God, if you would have eyes that see and ears that hear and a heart that understands, the wonders of life will begin to open unto you.

The choice is yours, and the responsibility begins with you. As Proverbs 1:20 says, *"Wisdom calls aloud outside; she raises her voice in the open squares"* (NKJV). An open door is set before you to choose life and to lay hold of the abundant life available to you. And it begins with giving no thought to the cares of the world but seeking first the Kingdom of God.

> Jesus said, "Take no thought" to the concerns of life. Give no place to worry, for it will only rob your life and leave nothing in its wake.

The Strength of
Your Life

Your attitude in life will determine much for you. It is much more important than you realize. Why? Because it will largely set the parameters for how far you go and how much you achieve. In other words, your attitude determines your attainment.

Consider Saint Paul. Paul was beaten multiple times with rods. He also received 39 stripes on his back because, according to the belief at the time, a human body could not absorb more and still live. Paul's back was a road map of scars. *"Five times I received at the hands of the Jews the forty lashes less one. Three times I was beaten with rods. Once I was stoned. Three times I was shipwrecked; a night and a day I was adrift at sea"* (2 Corinthians 11:24–25, ESV). For the sake of the Gospel, Paul endured more physical pain on his body than we recognize.

Here was a man who lived with persecution, who was imprisoned multiple times, and who would ultimately give his life for the Gospel. It is no small thing to be beaten, to be stoned, and to be left for dead. It should not be underestimated what it means to be shipwrecked, bitten by a deadly viper, and hated and hunted by the religious institution of the day.

All things considered, Paul had a right to worry. He had a right to feel the blues. No one would think less of him if he succumbed to the pressure after all he went through. But that was not Paul. And that's not you. He said, *"We are afflicted in every way, but not crushed; perplexed, but not despairing; persecuted, but not abandoned; struck down, but not destroyed"* (2 Corinthians 4:8–9, NASB).

Listen closely, you may be afflicted and you may be crushed, you may be persecuted and you may be struck down...but that is not the end of the story. Like Paul, you too have a Great High Priest who ever lives to make intercession for you. Like Paul, you can rise up, stand up, and keep going.

Let Paul's attitude also be found in you when he said, *"Rejoice in the Lord always; again I will say, rejoice"* (Philippians 4:4, ESV). Meaning, you can rejoice by choice. You can walk through the valley of the shadow of death. You can set your eyes on a Heavenly country and keep your hope on the Keeper of your soul.

Where is the strength of your life? The strength of your life is found in Christ and Christ alone. Paul had set his eyes on Heaven. He was not focused on the trials and tribulations he endured. His attitude was: *"For our light affliction, which is but for a moment, is working for us a far more exceeding and eternal weight of glory"* (2 Corinthians 4:17, NKJV). The trials or setbacks or hardships you are walking through right now do not define you and are not the ceiling of your life.

How then will you choose to live? What will be your attitude when it comes to afflictions, persecutions, and hardship? Set your face like flint and go out in the strength of the Lord. As for you, remember Paul's words: *"I can do all things through Christ who strengthens me"* (Philippians 4:13, NKJV).

Like Paul, you too have a Great High Priest who ever lives to make intercession for you. Like Paul, you can rise up, stand up, and keep going.

God With You

The fear of being alone. Transcending cultures, races, and national borders, it is seemingly a fundamental aspect of the human condition. A newborn baby in his mother's arms will cry and wail if he is set down because he does not want to be alone. A child dropped off for the first time will make a fuss because she does not want to be left alone. Throughout the teenage years and into young adulthood, a common thread is found — we do not want to be alone.

But Scripture provides a respite for our soul and a life preserver for the hope of our hearts. Found in the Torah, in one of the first five books of the Old Testament, God gives us a promise that will set the restlessness within to bed. He says, *"Be strong and of good courage, do not fear nor be afraid of them; for the LORD your God, He is the One who goes with you. He will not leave you nor forsake you"* (Deuteronomy 31:6, NKJV).

The God of the universe has said that He will not leave you nor forsake you. He is an Awesome God. He's an Almighty God. And He's an Ever-Present God. He is right there beside you, right now, able to lift your burden and solve your problems, to heal your sickness, and to make a way where there is no way. He can conquer your enemies, bring joy in the midst of sadness, and shine light into the darkest night of your life.

He is the One who is mighty to save, therefore you can rejoice and be exceedingly glad. He is with you. And if that is your God, why are you worried? If He will never forsake you, everything is going to work out all right. You can give the Lord mighty praise because He has said, *"He will never leave you nor forsake you."*

Why worry when you can pray? Why worry if God is on His throne? Why worry if the God that you serve cannot fail? Why worry if you walk through the fire and the fire won't burn you? Why worry if you walk through the water and the water can't drown you? God is bigger, stronger, and mightier than all.

Truly, you have no need to worry, for the God you serve is indeed the Creator of Heaven and earth. He is the One who flung the glittering stars against the velvet of the night. He is the One who is Almighty, All-Knowing, Sovereign, from Everlasting to Everlasting, the Alpha and the Omega, the Beginning and the End, the One who was and is and always shall be!

He never changes, and His heart towards you is steadfast. He can make a way where there is no way. He can provide when it seems all hope is lost. He can make beauty from ashes and bring water even from a rock. Saint Peter said: *"Casting all your care upon him; for he careth for you"* (1 Peter 5:7, KJV). When you cast your care upon God, you no longer are left to bear the burden. You can leave all at the foot of the Cross.

Before Jesus ascended to Heaven, He gave His disciples the Great Commission to go into all the world. And then He said, *"...And behold, I am with you always, to the end of the age"* (Matthew 28:20, ESV). Let Jesus' words guide you as you navigate every trial and tribulation. Think on them often, for no matter what, He has and will always be with you.

> When you cast your care upon God, you no longer are left to bear the burden. You can leave all at the foot of the Cross.

I Will Never
Leave You

Hear the Word of God today. Be comforted by it and changed forever, for the writer of Hebrews said: *"Never will I leave you; never will I forsake you." So we say with confidence, "The Lord is my helper; I will not be afraid. What can mere mortals do to me?"* (Hebrews 13:5–6, NIV). No matter what, God will never leave you.

We do not perhaps consider the picture of the shepherd and the sheep as we should. There is more for us to understand about the Father's heart to care for us in the depiction of the Good Shepherd. Only a loving God who is near, close, and cares would be known as a shepherd.

And that is the gift given to you: that your Heavenly Father is not only the Author and Perfecter of your faith but also One who leads you beside the still waters, restores your soul, and comforts you with His rod and staff. In the 1913 hymn, "In the Garden," the lyrics encourage us: *"And He walks with me, and He talks with me, and He tells me I am His own, and the joy we share as we tarry there, none other has ever known."* [viii]

Don't worry. Worry is contagious. It will start as a trickle in your thoughts, but just like a running stream, it will keep rushing and flowing until it carves out a furrow in your mind. It will not stop until you build a dam with the Word of God to hold back the incessant flow.

Saint Paul put it this way: *"...guard your hearts and minds in Christ Jesus. Finally, brothers and sisters, whatever is true, whatever is honorable, whatever is right, whatever is pure, whatever is lovely, whatever is commendable, if there is any excellence and if anything worthy of praise, think about these things"* (Philippians 4:7–8, NASB).

When the cares and concerns and worries of life come against you, you must guard your mind. You must combat them with truth. Hebrews 13:8 says that Jesus Christ is the same yesterday, today, and forever. He will never change, and He will never go back on His word.

If the Lord said, *"Never will I leave you; never will I forsake you,"* then that is truth that will never be shaken. Yesterday, He was with you. Right now, He is with you. And tomorrow, He will be with you. Psalm 139:7–10 says, *"Where shall I go from your Spirit? Or where shall I flee from your presence? If I ascend to heaven, you are there! If I make my bed in Sheol, you are there! If I take the wings of the morning and dwell in the uttermost parts of the sea, even there your hand shall lead me, and your right hand shall hold me"* (ESV). There is nowhere you can go that He will not also be there.

Rest in the promises of God. Rejoice with joy unspeakable and full of glory in the surpassing goodness of God in Heaven. In every battle, in every day, down to each moment, know beyond a shadow of a doubt that you are not alone, that God will never leave you, and that in Him, you can and will walk victorious because God Almighty is with you.

Hebrews 13:8 says that Jesus Christ is the same yesterday, today, and forever. He will never change, and He will never go back on His word.

No Faith in Fear

Make no mistake, there are absolute truths in life. There is right and wrong. There is good and evil. And when it comes to fear, you can refuse it or you can embrace it. But what happens when you embrace fear? When you embrace fear, you reject faith. Fear is the rejection of faith. If you are full of faith, fear has no place, but if you are full of fear, you will not operate in faith.

God, in His riches and mercy, has amply supplied you with everything you need to combat fear and lay hold of faith. Second Timothy 1:7 says, *"For God has not given us a spirit of fear, but of power and of love and of a sound mind"* (NKJV). God in Heaven has given you a spirit of power, love, and a sound mind. Armed with that cord of three strands, you can withstand the relentless onslaught of fear.

Have you ever noticed how worry comes at a bad time? It comes at a time when crisis is on the other side of the door. Just when you need a clear mind and creativity to make a wise decision, worry comes like an ominous cloud to cover the sun, draining you of the creative ability to think and land on the right solution for your problem.

Fear and worry go together. The fact is, fear is proof that the enemy has a foothold in your mind. Think about that. When trial or difficulty introduce themselves into your day, if your first impulse is to hold your breath and go to the worst-case scenario in your mind, then there is a stronghold of fear that you need to deal with. You must train yourself to cast down every fear and think of things that are noble and true.

Worry is trust in the unpleasant. It is assurance that disaster is coming. It is belief in defeat, despair, and that there is no hope for tomorrow. Worry is a polluted stream that flows through your mind and drowns every form of hope, optimism, and the good plan God has for you.

Don't let worry hamstring your faith. Worry is a barking dog behind a wall, it is a tornado warning of a storm that never appears, it is interest paid on trouble that never comes to pass. Worry has sidelined Bible-believing Christians, stolen destinies, and left nothing but torment and destruction in its wake.

Worry has no place in your life.

What did Paul say? He encouraged the church at Ephesus to be "strong in the Lord." Did you know that you have been thoroughly equipped with all you need for every good work? With the sword of the Spirit by your side, you are armed to the teeth for every spiritual battle. Ephesians 6:11–12 says, "*Put on the full armor of God, so that you can take your stand against the devil's schemes. For our struggle is not against flesh and blood, but against the rulers, against the authorities, against the powers of this dark world and against the spiritual forces of evil in the heavenly realms*" (NIV).

You must resist the enemy for him to flee. You must stand against his schemes. Don't let worry paralyze your mind. Don't let it rob your body of rest at night and you stumble into work the next day shattered, shaky, second-rate, and on the naked edge.
A life overshadowed by worry was never God's plan for you. Give fear none of your faith, rather, cast your faith on the shoulders of your Heavenly Father who loves you, is with you, and can do all things.

> Fear is the rejection of faith. If you are full of faith, fear has no place, but if you are full of fear, you will not operate in faith.

He Is Able

Whatever lack you have today, whatever need weighs heavy on your mind, whatever fear has an icy grip on your soul...please hear this immutable truth: The Lord is able. He is the One who is mighty to save. He is the One who created you, created the land you walk upon, and holds all things together by His word. For any problem on your mind, He is able.

He is able to aid you in your time of need. He is our merciful and faithful High Priest in all things pertaining to God. He is your provision in all things. *"For in that He Himself has suffered, being tempted, He is able to aid those who are tempted"* (Hebrews 2:18, NKJV). No temptation has overtaken you except that which is common to man. But He is faithful. He will provide a way out so you can endure it.

He is able to completely save you. He lives forever, and all things are under His feet. *"He is able to save to the uttermost those who draw near to God through him, since he always lives to make intercession for them"* (Hebrews 7:25, ESV). In Jesus, you have an Intercessor, an Advocate, and One who is able to save you. Find in Him your all in all.

He is able to do what must be done. He is able to do what only He can do. He is the slain Lamb who can stand at the center of the throne of God. John wrote, *"Then one of the elders said to me, 'Do not weep! See, the Lion of the tribe of Judah, the Root of David, has triumphed. He is able to open the scroll and its seven seals'"* (Revelation 5:5 NIV). He is All-Powerful! He is Almighty! He is the King of all.

Jesus Christ is able. The grand story of the Scripture points to one enduring theme over and over like a crimson cord woven from the pages of Genesis to Revelation, and it is that Jesus Christ is Lord, and He is Lord over all. He is seated on the throne. He is Worthy. He is Glorious. And for whatever is going on in your life, He is able to overcome and make a way.

Don't give in to worry. Don't give in to the cares and concerns of this life. As for you, raise your eyes and keep your gaze fixed on Heaven's horizon. God is enthroned forever. He is in charge, and everthing's going to be all right.

In the 1930s, Dr. Richard Niebuhr penned what has come to be known as "The Serenity Prayer." A popular version reads: *"God grant me the serenity to accept the things I cannot change; the courage to change the things I can, and the wisdom to know the difference."* [ix] The point is, don't worry about your life. Don't worry about what you can't change. But if there is something you can do to change what must, then go out and do it.

Remember, Jesus said, *"Which of you by worrying can add one cubit to his stature?"* (Luke 12:25, NKJV). Time given to worry will bear no fruit in your life. However, if you focus on the Word, on prayer, on giving God highest praise all throughout your day, your cares will begin to dim as you draw nearer and nearer to Him and find in Him all that you need.

He is the One who created you, created the land you walk upon, and holds all things together by His word. For any problem on your mind, He is able.

Section 3:

Fear Not

Fear. You'll find it splashed across the pages of your Bible. It is no small subject. From Genesis to Revelation, and from Abraham to John on the Isle of Patmos, we hear the command from Heaven ringing out over and over again: "Fear not! Fear not! Fear not!"

That command was given to Abraham. It was given to Moses. And it was given to Israel. It was given to David, to Daniel, and to the city of Jerusalem. The exhortation and command to not fear was given to the disciples as they were on the Sea of Galilee, to Mary when the angel Gabriel told her she would expect a child, and to the crowds who gathered to hear Jesus.

In Isaiah 41, God said it this way: *"Fear not, for I am with you; be not dismayed, for I am your God. I will strengthen you, yes, I will help you, I will uphold you with My righteous right hand"* (v. 10, NKJV). In Him we can find our strength, our help, and the One who will uphold us forever.

God has told us not to fear and not to be afraid. When God is with you, you cannot be defeated. When God is at your side, you can overcome all things. He is your source of strength, and He has promised to strengthen you. And He will strengthen you to do the work He has called you to do. All strength comes from God. He doesn't give it to you two hours before you need it. He gives it to you when you need it.

In God you will find all the help you need. You do not have to fear because God has said, *"I will help you."* He is your help in the little and in the large, in the mundane and in the magnitude. Remember Moses. God told Moses to lead an entire nation through the desert and to the Promised Land of Israel. But God did not leave him to it on his own. He parted the Red Sea, He supplied Manna from Heaven, and He Himself was a *"pillar of cloud to guide them on their way and by night in a pillar of fire to give them light"* (Exodus 13:21, NIV).

Do you need to be upheld today? Do you need a shoulder to lean upon? Rest in the unfailing promise of a faithful God: *"I will uphold you with My righteous right hand."* It is not all up to you. There is a reason why God has called Himself our Heavenly Father. He is not far removed, but closer than a brother. He is always right by your side. He will uphold you. He will bear you up. With His strong hand, He will carry you through.

Second Timothy 1 tells us that God has not given us a spirit of fear. Who you are on the inside is not a fearful person, because that is what the Bible says about you. Fear is a foreign entity that may work against you or that may come alongside you at times, but it is not who you are. God instead, has given you a spirit of power, of love, and of a mind that is sound.

Life can seem like mission impossible until God shows up saying, "I will help you." Appropriate the Word of God for your life. The message from Heaven for you to "Fear Not" is a powerful remedy to conquer storms and trials. Are you going through the most difficult moment of your life? I want you to make this confession today: "The Lord will help me!"

> God has told us not to fear and not to be afraid. When God is with you, you cannot be defeated.

What Is Fear?

Fear is a formidable foe. Fear is so powerful that it can change the course of entire nations. Just the dread of something that could happen is strong enough to shake us to our cores — even if the dreaded thing is unlikely in the extreme. Fear can be found everywhere. Yet it's important to distinguish between the common (and often commonsense) feeling of fear, and the "spirit of fear" that comes from the enemy.

These two types of fear are entirely different and have two distinct purposes. If you confuse them, you can put yourself in a state of condemnation. I want you to find out in the Word of God how they interact and work, because if you confuse one with the other, you can needlessly torment yourself.

Let's first examine the emotion of fear that God has built into all of us. A healthy fear can save you from perilous situations like stumbling upon a mountain lion on a wilderness trail or seeing a dorsal fin pop out of the water when you're swimming in the ocean. When you've been invited to pet a hungry alligator, the emotion you'll feel is likely well-founded. God gives you the emotion of fear to help you. It's hard-wired into you in the form of your "fight-or-flight response." A healthy fear can keep you alive.

The problem is not how to get rid of it, but how to bridle it to help, not hinder, you. Startle a rabbit in a thicket, and he bolts to save his life. Any deer that can't leap 10 feet out of an afternoon's nap and not come down with all four legs racing won't live through deer season.

In contrast, there is a spirit of fear that comes from the enemy that does nothing but steal from you. If there's something in your life over which you consistently carry paralyzing fear, that something is certainly not from the Lord. Fear that freezes you, keeps you from doing things you love, or robs your body of rest and your mind of peace, is an attack from the enemy.

Park your mind on 2 Timothy 1:7 and meditate on its words until they become a part of you: *"For God has not given us a spirit of fear, but of power and of love and of a sound mind"* (NKJV). According to that verse, right now, the gifts that God has given you include a spirit of power, a spirit of love, and the gift of a sound mind. These are truths for you straight from the Word of God.

If there is a fear in your life that controls you, it is vital to identify it and get rid of it. This kind of fear paralyzes the mind so that it cannot produce. Unnatural phobias that are abnormal, irrational, and mind-crippling are not from the Lord. They are a spirit of fear and do nothing but steal from your life.

What would you do if you had no fear? How would you live if you were completely fearless? Freedom from fear is found in God. You can combat fear. As a believer in Jesus Christ, you can say: "Though a host encamp against me, my heart shall not fear. Though war should rise against me, in the Lord will I be confident! For in the time of trouble, He shall hide me in His pavilion. In the secret of His tabernacle, He shall keep me safe. He shall lift up my head and set my feet on solid rock. My God is an awesome God!"

The gifts that God has given you include a spirit of power, a spirit of love, and the gift of a sound mind. These are truths for you straight from the Word of God.

Conquering Fear
With Faith

If you're looking for a sure-fire blueprint on how you can conquer fear, you will find it in a 5-letter word spelled F-A-I-T-H. Faith can conquer fear because faith is fear's opposite. What is faith? It is *"The substance of things hoped for, the evidence of things not seen"* (Hebrews 11:1, NKJV). Faith can move mountains, conquer kingdoms, administer justice, and gain what was promised (Hebrews 11:33). Faith can overcome fear any day of the week.

With each sunrise, you have a choice. You can approach your day in faith, or you can be conquered by fear before your feet hit the floor. You will either conquer fear or fear will conquer you. The presence of faith in your life is imperative for the Bible says, *"Without faith it is impossible to please Him, for he who comes to God must believe that He is, and that He is a rewarder of those who diligently seek Him"* (Hebrews 11:6, NKJV).

Faith is the gift of the believer that can bring you to victory. It has the power to overcome the world. Faith can look at the darkest cloud and say that rain is on the way. Faith starts out in assurance of the outcome because faith is completely confident in God's ability to bring His word to pass. By faith, you make a move before you know how it's going to turn out.

By faith, Noah prepared the ark and saved his household. By faith, Abraham left his homeland and received his inheritance from God. By faith, Sarah received strength in her body to bear the child of promise. By faith, Isaac blessed Jacob, Jacob blessed his sons, and Joseph made mention of the exodus of Israel from bondage in Egypt.

Faith drove Moses to declare to Pharaoh, *"Let my people go"* (Exodus 7:16, NIV), and by faith, they passed through the Red Sea as by dry land. By faith, the walls of Jericho fell down, and Joshua's armies conquered the Promised Land of Israel.

Faith drove David to face Goliath while an entire army cowered before him. David looked at that giant and said, *"You come to me with a sword and with a spear and with a javelin, but I come to you in the name of the LORD of hosts, the God of the armies of Israel, whom you have defied"* (1 Samuel 17:45, ESV). He wound up his slingshot, and the rock went forth and dropped the opposition in the name of God.

Please hear this: By faith you too can accomplish great feats in the name of the Lord. Faith has shut the mouths of lions, quenched the fury of the flames, and made a way of escape from the edge of the sword. Faith has turned weakness to strength, granted power in battle, and routed armies (Hebrews 11:33–34). By faith, you can conquer fear and accomplish the impossible.

The call is clear, and Heaven's admonition resounds like a trumpet saying: Fear not! Fear not! Fear not! Rather, have faith in God! Faith can turn your desert into a spring of living water. Faith can calm your troubled sea. Faith can move mountains of impossibility and create for you a stream in the wilderness. Faith is the victory that is available to you. Give God praise and glory!

> Faith starts out in assurance of the outcome because faith is completely confident in God's ability to bring His word to pass.

The Fear of
the Lord

There is only one truly "healthy" fear, and it is the fear of
the Lord. The Bible says that the fear of the Lord is the
beginning of wisdom. That with the fear of the Lord are
riches and honor and life (Proverbs 22:4). When we fear
the Lord, our lives fall into place. When we fear the Lord,
we depart from evil and run into the arms of our Heavenly Father, who loves us and can make all things work
together for our good.

Proverbs 1:7 says, *"The fear of the LORD is the beginning of knowledge"* (KJV). What is the fear of the
Lord? The fear of the Lord is knowing that God will
bring you into judgment if you do not obey Him.
That's an immense price to pay for disobedience.

The fear of the Lord will guard you, keep you,
and open the storehouses of wisdom over your life.
It is in the fear of the Lord that you will find the
answers you need and the keys to the problems
you face. King Jehoshaphat is a prime example.

When Jehoshaphat became king of Judah, he sought
God, followed God's commands, and walked in the
ways of David. Therefore, the Lord was with him. He

was courageous in the ways of the Lord and taught the people the Word of God. Because he feared God, the Lord established the kingdom of Judah in his hand. Second Chronicles 17:10–12 says, *"The fear of the LORD fell upon all the kingdoms of the lands that were around Judah, and they made no war against Jehoshaphat. Some of the Philistines brought Jehoshaphat presents and silver for tribute, and the Arabians also brought him 7,700 rams and 7,700 goats. And Jehoshaphat grew steadily greater"* (ESV). Many kings rose and fell in Judah and Israel, but Jehoshaphat grew great because he feared the Lord and walked in His commandments.

The fear of the Lord is not the same as the fear of consequences. You pay taxes not because you enjoy paying taxes but because you fear the consequences of not doing so. You take out car insurance, life insurance, and fire insurance not because you love sending extra money to your insurance agent but because you fear being wiped out by sudden tragedy. When the Titanic sank, many who were lucky enough to secure a spot in a lifeboat delayed returning to rescue those in the water for fear of being swamped themselves.[x] That is a different kind of fear.

To fear the Lord means to order your life around God's Word and God's ways. It means you believe what God has said and to act accordingly. It means you take seriously the 10 Commandments, the Lord's Prayer, and the exhortations of the Epistles.

When you do so, the blessings of God begin to flow in your life. Proverbs 10:27 says, *"The fear of the LORD prolongs life, but the years of the wicked will be short"*

(ESV). The fear of the Lord will prolong your life and give you good success in what you set your hand to do. It will do so because the fear of the Lord is pure and endures forever (Psalm 19:9). The fear of the Lord is of Heaven. It will beckon you to draw nearer and nearer still to the Good Shepherd of your soul, and when you do so, you will find life and life more abundant.

> To fear the Lord means to order your life around God's Word and God's ways.

Our Moral Nature

One of the greatest and most prevalent fears is "the fear of man." It's a term that describes excessively, obsessively concerning yourself with what other people think. When you let other people's opinions or the need for their approval drive you, you've given into the fear of man.

Proverbs 29:25 says, *"The fear of man brings a snare, but whoever trusts in the Lᴏʀᴅ shall be safe"* (NKJV). The fear of man will trap you and keep you in bondage. God planted the emotion of fear in your moral nature to make it uneasy for us to sin. The remedy is to fear God, keep His commandments, and tremble at His Word. When you fear God, you won't have the space to give into the fear of man or sin.

What do you give the energy of your thought life to? Do you meditate on Scripture, or do you create scenarios in your mind of all the things that could go wrong and why? Fear can become a self-fulfilling prophecy. If you fear greatly about something, you give it power to rule over you. You let it into your life and give it a license to take over.

What is the remedy? As for you, serve the Lord and rejoice before Him. Remember that He is a great God resplendent in glory and power. Psalm 2:10–12 says, *"Now therefore, be wise, O kings; be instructed, you judges of the earth. Serve the LORD with fear, and rejoice with trembling. Kiss the Son, lest He be angry, and you perish in the way, when His wrath is kindled but a little. Blessed are all those who put their trust in Him"* (NKJV). The key to find the path of life and not perish in the way is to trust in the Lord with all your heart.

Fear can rob you of your spiritual inheritance. Moses sent 12 spies into the Promised Land. Ten came back and said that there were giants everywhere, giants so big, they looked like grasshoppers. But Caleb said, *"We should by all means go up and take possession of it, for we will certainly prevail over it"* (Numbers 13:30, NASB). He said, "Let's get after it!"

Do you know what they wanted to do with Joshua and Caleb? They wanted to stone them. They didn't just want to silence the only two people who gave a good report; they wanted to go so far as to kill them for their testimony of faith and trust in the Lord. Times today have not changed much.

And we know what happened in the end. The result is that God let every man and woman in Israel from the age of 20 and up die in the wilderness. The only ones who would not die but would go on to inherit the Promised Land was Joshua and Caleb. Fear destroyed the spiritual inheritance of an entire generation. A generation that had seen the 10 plagues in Egypt, eaten Manna in the desert, and walked through the Red Sea.

An entire nation saw the power of God firsthand, but they let fear keep them from all the good things that God had planned for them. Don't let fear torment you, destroy your peace, or keep you from reaching your promised land. Strengthen your heart like Joshua and Caleb and believe with all your might that God can do all He said He could do.

> Don't let fear torment you, destroy your peace, or keep you from reaching your promised land.

No Fear
of God

In Matthew 10:28, Jesus said, *"Do not fear those who kill the body but cannot kill the soul. But rather fear Him who is able to destroy both soul and body in hell"* (NKJV). He cut straight to the chase. Do not fear man who can only do so much, but fear God who can destroy body and soul. God, His Word, and His commands will not be pushed aside.

Why should an unbeliever fear God? Because he or she will wind up in Hell if they don't, where the worm dieth not and the fire is never quenched (Mark 9:44). God is not sitting benignly in the Heavens. He's not saying, "Let's make a deal" to rebellious, reprobate mankind. He's saying, "This is the deal. I am the Judge of all the earth. And you are going to answer to Me in the day of judgment. You are going to give an account for every word, every thought, and every deed." One day, we will all give an account for our lives. That is a foreign thought in the American mindset, but He is still God, and we're going to answer to Him.

Why is a woman assaulted every day in America? There's no fear of God whatsoever. If a rapist tru-ly believed he was going to face God and answer for his actions, he wouldn't go near that woman. Why is this nation saturated with murder, crime, immorality, and corruption? There is no fear of God.

Every day, we see people consumed with love for themselves and love for money. All around, people are *"boastful, proud, abusive, disobedient to their parents, ungrateful, unholy, without love, unforgiving, slanderous, without self-control, brutal, not lovers of the good, treacherous, rash, conceited, lovers of pleasure rather than lovers of God"* (2 Timothy 3:2–4, NIV). And all of it begins with rejecting the fear of God.

We have thrown the 10 Commandments out of public school, and we have rejected prayer in the classroom. Greed and corruption run rampant in government offices, and we have yet to atone for the scourge of 50 years of abortion. All the while, preachers have abandoned the Word of God as the absolute authority of the believer. Why? Because there's no fear of God. I assure you; judgment day is coming.

Jesus describes what the end of the age will be like for those who do not believe: *"The angels will come and separate the wicked from the righteous and throw them into the blazing furnace, where there will be weeping and gnashing of teeth"* (Matthew 13:49–50, NIV). This will be the story for those who do not fear God and never gave their will over to the Lordship of Jesus Christ.

Revelation 21:8 says, *"But the cowardly, unbelieving, abominable, murderers, sexually immoral, sorcerers, idolaters, and all liars shall have their part in the lake which burns with fire and brimstone, which is the second death"* (NKJV). What we need to understand is that the human soul is immortal and there is a real lake of fire.

God is a real God, there's a real eternity, and we will answer to Him. Believers who know the Word of God have an awesome respect for the Lord and reverently and joyously live by it. The Word of the Living God will last forever. Fear God, read the Bible, and seek the Lord. In Him is the path of life.

> Believers who know the Word of God have an awesome respect for the Lord and reverently and joyously live by it.

Every Knee

God has highly exalted Jesus. He has given Him the name which is above every name in Heaven and on earth. Nothing can stand before the name of Jesus. Philippians 2:10–11 says, *"That at the name of Jesus every knee should bow, of those in heaven, and of those on earth, and of those under the earth, and that every tongue should confess that Jesus Christ is Lord, to the glory of God the Father"* (NKJV).

It's not a matter of if you're going to bow. It's a matter of when you're going to bow. Every knee will bow one day before the King of kings and Lord of lords. That means every person throughout history and all who are alive today. No one will escape that day, but every single person will bow and confess that Jesus Christ is Lord.

It is an awesome thing to consider that one day you will bow before Jesus. If you believe that is true, how are you ordering your life today? Are you preparing for that day? Do you think of that day with joyful expectation to finally be face-to-face with your Lord, or does the mere thought of it fill you with dread? Prepare yourself today, for one day you will meet God.

Set God first above all else. Matthew 22:37 says, *"You shall love the Lord your God with all your heart and with all your soul and with all your mind"* (ESV). That means God takes precedent over everything in your life. That means you love God more than you love yourself. That means you take your heart, mind, and soul — all that you are — and you love God first and foremost.

How do you view your Bible? Do you tremble at God's Word? Psalm 119:120 says, *"My flesh trembles for fear of You, and I am afraid of Your judgments"* (NKJV). Do not handle lightly the very words of God. For in them are the words of life, but to disdain them leads to destruction. Esteem the Word of God. Meditate on the Word of God. Let the Word of God be the plumbline and standard by which you live your life.

Today, confess that the Lord is your help and the strength of your life. Come to Him for every need and problem that you are facing and declare that He is King and Lord over all things in your life. In Him, find victory today. In Him, claim the promises of God. Live as a son or daughter of the King, as one who has become the righteousness of God in Christ Jesus by faith and declare that the Lord is with you.

Every knee will bow before Him because He is the mighty God. He is the Creator of Heaven and earth. He who flung the stars against the darkness of the night. He who is the Alpha and the Omega, the First and the Last. He who is the Cornerstone and the Precious Elect of Zion. He is Immanuel, God with us. He is our Fortress. He is our High Tower. He is our Shield and our Buckler.

He is Jehovah Shammah, the Lord who is there. He is Jehovah Rophe, the God that heals all our diseases. He is the Almighty, All-Knowing, All-Powerful, resurrected Son of God. He is Heaven's hope and Hell's dread. He is the Lord of glory. He is the Lion of Judah. He is the Light of the World. Fear not! The Lord will help you. Give Him praise and glory today, for one day you will stand before Him.

> Let the Word of God be the plumbline and standard by which you live your life.

God's Word Will
Not Fail

In Exodus 20, God gave Israel the 10 Commandments. The first commandment is this: *"You shall have no other gods before me"* (v. 3, NIV). Anything you place above God can become a god to you. Anything that you give more time, energy, effort, and focus can take an idolatrous place in your life. Giving into fear and letting your schedule and decisions be consumed or managed by fear means fear has taken up residence and has become an idol.

You must renounce fear and lay claim to the promises of God. You must appropriate the Word of God for every area of your life to defeat fear and move forward in God's plans for you. The Bible says you have a loving Heavenly Father who has a purpose and a plan for your life. It says that in Him, you can do all things through Christ, and that nothing is impossible to those who believe.

If a child's father makes a promise, is it presumptuous of the child to believe the father? No. The child believes the word of the father because the child takes the father at his word. The child believes simply and completely and does not presume to doubt.

The promises of God are absolutely true, and God keeps His covenant of His Word and of His love for a thousand generations with those who love Him and keep His commandments (Deuteronomy 7:9). You are what the Word of God says you are. You can have what it says you can have, and you can do what it says you can do. Believe on the Word of God.

And what does the Bible say? Jesus said, *"All things are possible to him who believes"* (Mark 9:23, NKJV). That verse can change your life if you'll let it. All you have to do is believe. Believe that what the Bible says is true and that you can cause your life to come into alignment with the words of the Bible.

David said, *"Yea, though I walk through the valley of the shadow of death, I will fear no evil; for You are with me; Your rod and Your staff, they comfort me"* (Psalm 23:4, NKJV). The 23rd Psalm is perhaps the most well-known psalm in the Bible. Maybe you've quoted it before, but the question is not whether or not you know it by memory but whether or not you believe it.

Joshua said, *"Be strong and courageous. Do not be frightened, and do not be dismayed, for the LORD your God is with you wherever you go"* (Joshua 1:9, ESV). God's command in this text is to not fear and to not be dismayed. God does not say, "Do not fear often." He doesn't say that. He says, "Do not fear, period. I will not fail you. I will be there. If I promised it, I will deliver it because I am a faithful God." Rather than focusing on your fear, give God praise and glory and watch the enemy flee.

He can grant favor and honor where you need it. He can turn the hearts of kings. Psalm 84:11 says, *"The LORD God is a sun and shield; the LORD bestows favor and honor; no good thing does he withhold from those whose walk is blameless"* (NIV). Many fear being alone. But God the Father is with you. Jesus Christ is with you. The angels of God are walking in front of you and behind you. The Holy Spirit has anointed you. The Lord is your shield; you are never alone, and in Him you can find all you need.

The promises of God are absolutely true, and God keeps His covenant of His Word and of His love for a thousand generations with those who love Him and keep His commandments (Deuteronomy 7:9).

The Spirit of Fear

I have thoroughly researched that Hebrew word translated "fear." Would you like to know what I discovered about its meaning? It means: fear. There is a spirit of fear that is pervasive in the world, and it comes from the enemy. The spirit of fear comes from Satan, the prince of darkness. Think about that phrase "prince of darkness." When you choose to live in darkness, Satan is your prince. "Prince" means someone who has authority. So, when you are living in sin and rebellion, Satan has the authority to run your life. When you reject darkness, then you walk in the light as Christ is in the light, and you have the joy of following Jesus — the Light of the World.

There are only two kingdoms represented on earth today. There is the kingdom of darkness and the kingdom of light. You live in the kingdom that you wish to live in by choice. If you're in the kingdom of darkness, Satan is your master. You have no free choice. He rules you, reigns over you, and drags you around on the end of a rope.

And his chief taskmaster is fear. Disease may have killed its thousands, but fear has killed its tens of thousands. Your greatest crisis will come not from the presence of trouble but from the fear of trouble.

The spirit of fear will break your spirit. The spirit of fear that comes from the prince of darkness will destroy your mind. It will destroy your defenses. It only brings terror and destruction because the enemy prowls around like a lion, seeking whom he may devour. He only steals, kills, and destroys.

Regardless of your profession of faith, if you have the spirit of fear, you are, in a practical sense, an atheist. I've seen hundreds of people die, perhaps thousands. But I have never seen a believer die who had an ounce of fear because they knew that beyond that last breath was the face of God. And I have never seen the ungodly die with peace because they knew beyond that last breath were the gates of Hell.

If there is a spirit of fear within you, a part of you is being influenced by the prince of darkness. But you don't have to be. Second Timothy 1:7 says, *"For God has not given us a spirit of fear, but of power and of love and of a sound mind"* (NKJV). That spirit of fear did not come from God, and you don't have to live with it. You can resist the enemy and watch him flee.

The Lord has good plans for you. He has plans for your welfare and your peace. He is the One who will empower you with strength for the fight and hope for the day. God said, *"So do not fear, for I am with you; do not be dismayed, for I am your God. I will strengthen you and help you; I will uphold you with my righteous right hand"* (Isaiah 41:10, NIV). That is a verse you can take to the bank.

You need to know who you are. You are not of this world. No, you are a son or a daughter of God. You have been adopted and chosen and brought near to God. Consider the words of Paul that are true for you today: *"For all who are being led by the Spirit of God, these are sons and daughters of God. For you have not received a spirit of slavery leading to fear again, but you have received a spirit of adoption as sons and daughters by which we cry out, 'Abba! Father!'"* (Romans 8:14–15, NASB). Adoption, freedom, and sonship are who you are.

> The Lord has good plans for you. He has plans for your welfare and your peace.

When Fear Attacks!

Fear was not God's original plan for humankind. But it entered man's soul in the garden of Eden as a product of sin. Adam was never afraid of God until he sinned by taking the forbidden fruit. Adam walked with God in the garden. He talked with God as a child speaks with his father. Unashamed and unafraid. But when Adam sinned, *"The LORD God called unto Adam, and said unto him, Where art thou?"* (Genesis 3:9, KJV), and fear entered the world for the first time.

When God asks a question, He's not looking for information. He has the answers. He knows. He knew that fear had already attacked Adam and Eve's emotions. He knew their disobedience had already begun working death in them, just as He had warned. Yes, He warned them, but they disobeyed and were expelled from paradise. Fear will destroy you. It will attack your mind, it will attack your body, and it will continually bring up your past. In doing so, it will fill you with shame and dread.

Sin is the mother of the spirit of fear that torments you. The spirit of fear continues in men because sin continues to rule their lives. Fear comes into the heart by sin. It is then sustained by repeated sin. Like an infection, it invades the soul, continually causing the person to return to their sin so that it might continue to live. Sin gives fear a license to rule over your family, your marriage, your business, and your life. Sin keeps you coming back for more because every time you do, its power grows in your life.

Fear will relentlessly attack your mind and say, "You're too tired to try again. You're too exhausted to endure. You're too weak to win. Just give up." But fear only speaks in lies. You must shout back in faith, "No! I am more than a conqueror through Christ, and nothing is impossible with God!"

You gain the strength to fight fear by continually returning to find refuge under the wings of the Lord. Isaiah 40:31 says, *"But they that wait upon the Lord shall renew their strength; they shall mount up with wings as eagles; they shall run, and not be weary; and they shall walk, and not faint"* (KJV). If you are out there fighting fear like a lone ranger, eventually you will fall. But if you wait upon the Lord and call upon God for your every need, you will renew your strength. In Him you will find victory over fear's attack.

Fear will bring up your past and accuse you. It will say that God will never forgive you for what you did or forget the sin you've done. But that is totally contrary to the Word of God. Faith shouts back, *"Where sin abounded, grace abounded much more"* (Romans 5:20, NKJV). That means God's grace is greater than all your sin.

You may have been a professional sinner, but the grace of God is greater still. John Newton, the man who penned

"Amazing Grace," was once a slave trader. He lived a life of sin before repenting of his ways and turning to God.[xi]

You may have gone all out and even committed murder. Did you know that David killed Uriah the Hittite, Moses killed the Egyptian who was beating the Israelite slave, and Paul consented to the death of Stephen? Guess what? They're all in Heaven right now because they repented and God's grace is greater than any sin on earth. No matter what you've done or how far you've gone, you can always repent and turn once again to God. God's grace is greater still.

> You gain the strength to fight fear by continually returning to find refuge under the wings of the Lord.

The Strongest
Men

The Bible tells us of champions in the faith. We read of men and women who walked with God, accomplished great things, and whose very lives are canonized in Scripture. Yet even the strongest men in the Bible also dealt with the same fears and anxieties that are common to us today.

Through faith and courage, Elijah conquered 450 prophets of Baal on Mount Carmel (1 Kings 18). When he prayed, the fire of God fell from Heaven and consumed the burnt offering before all of Israel. Moreover, Elijah then prayed for rain, and a downpour came over the land. But in the very next chapter, Jezebel threatens him, and Elijah runs off into the wilderness, sits down under a juniper tree, and asked God to take his life.

On the night Jesus was arrested, Peter and John followed the mob to the high priest's courtyard. John spoke to the servant girl to bring Peter in, but before she would, she asked Peter, *"You also are not one of this man's disciples, are you?"* (John 18:17, ESV). Then and there, Peter denied Jesus for what would be the first of three times that night.

If you know the first thing about theology, you know that in Matthew 10:33, Jesus said, *"Whoever denies Me before men, him I will also deny before My Father who is in heaven"* (NKJV). Peter's soul was hanging over the fires of Hell by a thread. He had denied Christ three times. But even so, in His abundant mercy and grace, Jesus would forgive, restore, and empower Peter once again.

Remember that God is greater than your fear. Remember that with God on your side, you can do great and mighty things. God's strength poured into Samson, and he carried the gates of Gaza to the top of a hill. God's strength poured into David, and he defeated a lion, a bear, and Goliath in the Valley of Elah.

You never know how God will show up. He can even use a bush in the wilderness. When Moses saw the burning bush, it was worthless. It was an ecological nonentity. It had no beauty. But the angel of the Lord appeared in a blazing fire from the midst of the bush, the bush raged with fire, and Moses said, *"I must turn aside and see this marvelous sight, why the bush is not burning up!"* (Exodus 3:3, NASB). God spoke to Moses out of that bush, and Moses went to Egypt and set the Jewish people free.

God used a bush to talk to Moses, He used a donkey to talk to Balaam, and He used a fish to pay the temple tax for Jesus and Peter. Recognize that the Lord is with you today. You are well able and equipped to do all that God has for you to do. Right now, you have enough power to make demons in hell tremble with fear because *"He who is in you is greater than he who is in the world"* (1 John 4:4, ESV).

Don't allow fear to drive you. Give no place for fear to have any control in your life. With God, you can fulfill your spiritual destiny. Reject doubt, reject fear, and reject the spirit of the age. Remember Jesus' words when He said, *"All things are possible for the one who believes"* (Mark 9:23, NASB).

> Recognize that the Lord is with you today. You are well able and equipped to do all that God has for you to do.

A Deadly Profile!

Fear is a silent killer. Fear is why the Israelites listened to the 10 spies instead of Joshua and Caleb and consequently died in the wilderness. The report of only 10 men was enough to sway an entire nation. Fear is contagious. It spreads on the wings of doubt and destroys like the plague.

Fear will tell you that your business is going to fail, but Deuteronomy 8:18 says, *"You shall remember the LORD your God, for it is he who gives you power to get wealth, that he may confirm his covenant that he swore to your fathers, as it is this day"* (ESV). When fear rears its head, you must claim the promises of God.

Fear will tell you that the disease in your body is fatal, but faith shouts back, *"I shall not die, but live, and declare the works of the LORD"* (Psalm 118:17, NKJV). Faith says, "By His stripes, I am healed." By faith, you can overcome the words of the enemy when fear comes accusing. Find a Scripture and say, "It is written..."

No matter what the world may say, Jesus Christ is still the Great Physician. He is the One who can heal and bring restoration to your mind, body, and soul. James 5:14 says, *"Is anyone among you sick? Then he must call for the elders of the church and they are to pray over him, anointing him with oil in the name of the Lord"* (NASB). Apply the Word of God that is living and active to any area of need or lack.

Fear is not your story. You are a child of God. You are an ambassador of the Lord Jesus Christ. You cannot be defeated. You need to take up the sword of the Spirit and live by faith in the Word of God over every fear. It is up to you to take charge of your life. Fear not! God is with you.

Settle in your mind once and for all that because of what Jesus has done, when you place your faith in Him, you are washed white as snow. One thing God will not do is remember sin that has been washed in the blood of the Cross. When you are washed, you are clean before God. Your sin is forgiven, and it's forgotten. Psalm 103:11–12 says, *"For as high as the heavens are above the earth, so great is his love for those who fear him; as far as the east is from the west, so far has he removed our transgressions from us"* (NIV). Now if God has forgotten it, you can forget it as well.

The One who is mighty to save is with you. And He can bring about His good purposes in your life. Third John 1:2 says, *"Beloved, I pray that all may go well with you and that you may be in good health, as it goes well with your soul"* (ESV). He can make all things go well with you.

Your prescription is to do as David did. He said, *"Blessed is the man who walks not in the counsel of the ungodly, nor stands in the path of sinners, nor sits in the seat of the scornful; but his delight is in the law of the LORD, and in His law he meditates day and night.*

He shall be like a tree planted by the rivers of water,
that brings forth its fruit in its season, whose leaf also
shall not wither; and whatever he does shall prosper"
(Psalm 1:1–3, NKJV). That's the Word of God. If
you would conquer the spirit of fear, all that is left
for you to do is lay claim to the promises of God.

> One thing God will not do
> is remember sin that has
> been washed in the blood
> of the Cross. When you
> are washed, you are
> clean before God.

Section 4:

Control Thyself

Survey the world today and you'll find many Christians but precious few disciples. In John 8:31, Jesus said, *"If you abide in My word, you are My disciples indeed"* (NKJV). If you want to be a disciple of Jesus, abide in the Word of God. When you do what's in the Word, when you discipline yourself to live by the words of the Bible, and when you abide in the Word of God, then you are living the life of a disciple.

Now if you look at the word "discipline," you can see the word disciple. If you are not a disciple and if you are not disciplined, who are you? You may have come to Christ, confessed your sin, and even been baptized in the Jordan River, but you're not a disciple until you do what Jesus asks you to do. You can be saved but still do nothing in the Kingdom of God.

We are an instant gratification generation. We want what we want, we want it right now, and we don't want anything or anyone to prevent us from having what we want. Many hate the word discipline because it means they have to do something they don't want to do or deny themselves something they do want. Discipline is usually not pleasant at the time, but it produces results that are.

We can't just believe; we also have to go out and do something. Jesus said, *"Why do you call me, 'Lord, Lord,' and do not do what I say?"* (Luke 6:46, NIV). It is not enough to call Jesus "Lord." We are His disciples when we do what He has asked of us. Until you are doing what Jesus asks of you, you are not disciplined. You're a wild horse doing your own thing, not advancing the Kingdom of God.

In this age of advanced technology, it's easier for a man to control the universe than to control himself. We have learned to control everything but ourselves. We control the sun to heat our houses. We control mighty rivers to produce electricity for our cities. We control satellites in space to transmit communication signals all over the world. We control deadly diseases with wonder drugs. But in all of our technological advances, we have not learned how to control ourselves.

Paul said, *"I do not run aimlessly; I do not box as one beating the air. But I discipline my body and keep it under control, lest after preaching to others I myself should be disqualified"* (1 Corinthians 9:26–27, ESV). There is a call of God on your life because you are God's handiwork. You do not need to run through life aimlessly or unduly. He created you in Christ Jesus to do good works, which He prepared in advance for you to do. That means there are specific things out there that will bless the Kingdom of God and fill you with contentment, and they have your name on them.

How will you complete those good works? They will not fall into your lap; you have to run with purpose, discipline your body, and keep moving forward to complete them. It might mean you sit down and make a plan, outlining the steps you need to take. It might mean you find wise counsel on what you need to do. The point is that you do something to complete the good things that the Lord has prepared for you.

> When you do what's in the Word, when you discipline yourself to live by the words of the Bible, and when you abide in the Word of God, then you are living the life of a disciple.

Dream Traitors

Men the world over and throughout history have searched for ways to control themselves. The ancient Spartans gave themselves to rigorous military regiments to subject their bodies to training; the Stoics believed that good only came in virtue; and even Socrates, Plato, and Aristotle each taught on the value and need for self-control. It has been a topic on the forefront of thought for most civilizations.

One such school of philosophy was "self-assertion." Self-assertion gave free rein to any and every natural impulse. They are natural, therefore, they're self-justified. It feels good, so it must be good. Have you ever heard that before?

Self-assertion would say that whatever is natural is beautiful. And if it's beautiful, it must be right. The only sin in this philosophy was to suppress those natural desires. Some call it "the new morality," but it's not new and it's not moral; it's idolatry.

Nietzsche, the philosopher of Germany, taught self-assertion. Nietzsche taught that man should be strong, assertive, and a superman. He said to throw off pious priests and their weak-livered gospel of mercy and purge the soul of this devil called Christianity.

Rather, develop a master race of supermen. Perhaps his most well-known quote was "God is dead."[xii]

Adolf Hitler believed Nietzsche to the core. He believed in the mastery of the strong man and the production of the super race. What did it produce? It produced Dachau, Auschwitz, and Birkenau. Six million Jewish people were systematically murdered, and 50 million people died around the world because one man, Hitler, listened to Nietzsche, who said that man should be left free to do whatever he wishes and instinctually pursue his own objectives.

Proverbs 14:12 says, *"There is a way which seemeth right unto a man, but the end thereof are the ways of death"* (KJV). God said that long ago, and had humanity followed it, millions upon millions of people would not have died untimely deaths throughout history. But there was no fear of God, and people were left to run their lives unrestrained, and it produced hell on earth.

In 1973, when the U.S. Supreme Court issued its *Roe v. Wade* ruling, it constituted a death sentence for millions of Americans. For roughly 50 years, abortion reigned free until the decision was overturned. It is now up to the states to decide if a baby in a mother's womb is a baby with a right to life. I want you to understand that in the Word of God, a baby in the womb is precious. There is life in a woman's womb, and to take it is tantamount to murder before the throne of God. It was the same philosophy: do what you want with no concern for others.

We must teach our children that there is right and wrong and there is good and evil. There is a God in Heaven who will be magnified and glorified and honored. We must return to the Word of

God as the foundation for every rule of life. Only then will we find the true peace that we seek.

> We must return to the Word of God as the foundation for every rule of life.

A Most
Valuable Lesson

Embracing the virtue of discipline is one of the Bible's most valuable lessons. Discipline is the ability to make yourself do the things you have to do when they must be done. Discipline is doing what you need to do with excellence, whether you want to do it or not. Discipline may very well be one of the most important lessons this generation needs to learn.

Discipleship is costly. The Christian life is not easy. Jesus said, *"If anyone wants to come after Me, he must deny himself, take up his cross, and follow Me. For whoever wants to save his life will lose it; but whoever loses his life for My sake will find it"* (Matthew 16:24–25, NASB). What are you denying yourself? What cross do you bear? We must seek God first and above all else.

Life is not about doing what you want all the time. The world does not revolve around you, and there is serious work to complete. Before Jesus ascended to Heaven, He said, *"Go therefore and make disciples of all nations, baptizing them in the name of the Father and of the Son and of the Holy Spirit, teaching them to observe all that I have commanded you"* (Matthew 28:19–20, ESV). The Great Commission is yet to be completed.

Life is not about doing what you want to do all the time. Jesus said that we would only find our lives when we lose them for the sake of the Gospel. We must deny ourselves and get busy doing the work the Lord has set before us. Then we will find enjoyment, fulfillment, and contentment in our work and lives.

It has been quoted, "Boys do what they want, men do what they must." That's discipline. Do you have it? Do you do what you must? You may be brilliant, but without discipline, you're finished. You may be wealthy, but without discipline, poverty will overtake you. You may be powerful, but without discipline, you'll lose it all. Your life and your career are already over.

You and you alone are responsible for what you do to God and man. And one day you will answer for who you are and what you have or haven't done. What will the *magnum opus* of your life be? What will be written in your obituary? Will they say of you that you loved the Lord with all your heart, soul, mind, and strength? Or will they say you were merely a nice person to be around?

You must come after Christ with all that you have and all that you are. The life of the believer is a life of discipleship. It is a constant adherence to the path that is straight and narrow and leads to life. You cannot have one foot in the world and the other in the church. The call to follow Christ is a call for total commitment with no looking back.

In *The Cost of Discipleship*, Bonhoeffer said, "Jesus summons men to follow Him not as a teacher or a pattern of the good life, but as the Christ, the Son of God."[xiii] To follow

Jesus is not a part-time pledge. It is a call to come and die, once and for all. But when you lay your life down at the foot of the Cross, only then will you begin to truly live.

The call to follow Christ is a call for total commitment with no looking back.

The Battle for
Self-Control

Discipline is one of the most important words in your vocabulary. You know the word, but you need to spend time thinking about what it means because discipline is demanded of the believer. And the more disciplined you are now, the better your life will be later. Discipline can save your life.

Do you have self-control? Can you say no to yourself and make yourself do the things you need to do, even when you don't feel like it? Can you harness your passions and deny your body the sugar it craves or the sleep it cries out for, to give yourself to fasting, weeping, and mourning? Are you in control of yourself, or do the trappings of the world determine your every decision?

You'd better find a way to bring discipline and self-control into your life because without them, you won't keep the good things you do have, and you are on a path to poverty, destruction, and the grave. Proverbs 16:32 says, *"One who is slow to anger is better than the mighty, and one who rules his spirit, than one who captures a city"* (NASB). That means the one who rules their spirit and has self-control is greater than the one who conquers an entire city.

You need self-control to live the Christian life. Christianity is both a discipline and a doctrine. It is something you believe, and it is something you do. Only believing that God exists is not enough to fulfill the requirements of maturing in your walk with the Lord. The demons in Hell believe God exists. James 2:19 says, *"You believe that God is one. You do well; the demons also believe, and shudder"* (NASB). They believe in God; they just don't obey Him. It's very important to understand the difference.

Saint Paul taught that salvation comes through faith. Ephesians 2:8 says, *"For by grace you have been saved through faith, and that not of yourselves; it is the gift of God"* (NKJV). You are saved by grace. And you are saved through faith. Yet even faith itself is a gift. That's important as a doctrine to believe.

But Paul also said, *"I discipline my body and bring it into subjection, lest, when I have preached to others, I myself should become disqualified"* (1 Corinthians 9:27, NKJV). Paul was not wishy-washy when it came to doing what needed to be done. He brought his body into subjection that he might do the will of God for his life. That's discipline. You need to hear the Word, believe the Word, and do the Word.

Christians are expected to demonstrate discipline in every capacity of their lives. You're supposed to discipline yourself in your passions, in your affections, in your thoughts, and in your attitudes. You need discipline in your moods, in your speech, in your conduct, and in your habits. Discipline is necessary in your relationships, in your purpose, and in your marriage. There is no subject or area of life where you do not need discipline.

Remember, Proverbs says that the man who conquers himself is greater than the one who conquers a mighty city. The first step is total reliance on God. What is impossible for man is possible for God. And you have the Holy Spirit, the Helper and Paraclete, who will help guide you into the paths of righteousness. If you seek self-control, begin by calling on the Lord in faith believing that He will lead you, guide you, and help you.

> Christianity is both a discipline and a doctrine. It is something you believe, and it is something you do.

Rigorous Training

Discipline can change your life. In society today, discipline is a word we love to hate. Yet we must bring it into our lives if we are to be successful in any endeavor. If we are to grow in spiritual matters, we must discipline ourselves to read the Word, believe the Word, and obey the Word of God. Without discipline, we will never fulfill the good plans God has for us.

I was watching the Olympics one day. I watched those magnificent athletes with awe, each striving to win a gold medal. When one of them won gold, I listened as he described to the world how he subjected himself to intense discipline. He disciplined his appetite. He guarded every hour of rest. He put himself through a rigorous, back-breaking exercise routine hour after hour, day after day, week after week, and year after year. Why did he go to such great lengths? All of it was so that for those four or five minutes, he was on center stage before the world. So that for one moment, he could be the absolute best the world had ever seen.

If an Olympic athlete will spend that kind of energy to be successful for four or five minutes to win one gold medal, can we do less in the Kingdom of God? There are only so many hours in a day, so many days in a year, and so many years we each will live. It is time to get busy with Kingdom work. It is time to do what we can to win the lost and present the Gospel to all the world that they may know Jesus Christ, who is Savior and Lord of all.

Jesus demanded discipline of His disciples. When He walked by the shore of the Sea of Galilee and called His disciples, He did not say, "When you're ready and when it's convenient, come find Me." He said, *"Follow Me"* (Matthew 4:19, NKJV). When they heard those words, immediately Peter and Andrew, and James and John left their boats and their nets and followed Jesus.

In 5th century Britain, a young 16-year-old boy was taken captive from his home in England and lived as a slave in Ireland for six years. He eventually escaped back to his homeland and entered the ministry. He would return to Ireland as a missionary and spread Christianity far and wide. By the 7th century, St. Patrick was known as the patron saint of Ireland. In a prayer known as St. Patrick's Breastplate, we read, *"Christ with me, Christ before me, Christ behind me, Christ in me, Christ beneath me, Christ above me..."*[xiv] We know who St. Patrick is today because he lived a life of self-control, principle, and discipline.

The message is that if you would be a disciple of Christ, you must serve as Jesus did. You must lay down your life for the sake of the Gospel. Only servants are disciples. If you cannot serve, you cannot be a disciple. There are no superstars in the Kingdom of God. We are all servants of God. When you get to Heaven, the words you will long to hear are, *"Well done, thou good and faithful servant: thou hast been faithful over a*

few things, I will make thee ruler over many things: en-
ter thou into the joy of thy lord" (Matthew 25:21, KJV).

The call to follow Christ is no small thing. Listen to Jesus: *"If anyone would come after me, let him deny him-self and take up his cross and follow me"* (Matthew 16:24, ESV). You must set your face like flint if you would take up the call of God on your life and follow Him whole-heartedly. Who knows what good things the Lord has for you to do if you would but launch out into the deep?

> If we are to grow in spiritual matters, we must discipline ourselves to read the Word, believe the Word, and obey the Word of God.

The Demand
of Discipline

Can you control yourself? Do you rule over the passions of your body and soul? In the battle for self-control, the enemy is you. The war of the soul is a civil war that wages on the inside of the heart. You may be successful at making money, building a business, being a great leader of people, or athletic prowess, but if you cannot control yourself, you're already finished.

Saint Paul wrote, *"Every man that striveth for the mastery is temperate in all things"* (1 Corinthians 9:25, KJV). Temperate is another word for self-control. Ability will help you win a game, but discipline will win a championship. Ability may get you to the top, but discipline will keep you there. The word "temperance" means discipline, and it is temperance that will set you apart.

In April 1945, the 307th Infantry, 77th Infantry Division of the US Army was stationed near Urasoe Mura, Okinawa. The battalion was tasked with scaling a 400-foot cliff, nicknamed Hacksaw Ridge, to engage in battle on a plateau. Within the ranks was a man of unbelievable discipline. His name was Pfc. Desmond Doss, and he served as a medic and noncombatant.

After an assault, the entire American force was driven down the ridge, leaving only Pfc. Doss to treat the wounded. Over the course of several hours, he would drag wounded men to the ridge and lower them down on a rope. Each time, he prayed, "Dear God, let me get just one more man."[xv] For saving the lives of close to 100 men, he received the Medal of Honor.

Self-control is listed among the fruit of the Spirit. *"The fruit of the Spirit is love, joy, peace, longsuffering, kindness, goodness, faithfulness, gentleness, self-control. Against such there is no law"* (Galatians 5:22–23, NKJV). If you would live a life that is in line with the principles of God's Kingdom on earth, study the lists of these nine attributes and make them part of your daily life.

Not every race is won in the first lap, but the runner who endures throughout the race will lift the victor's crown. Many football games are won in the fourth quarter not because they are more skilled, but because the team that was the most disciplined in the offseason and trained and built endurance is the team that has the strength to continue playing hard at the end of the game.

Do you have discipline in your life? Proverbs 10:17 says, *"Whoever heeds discipline shows the way to life"* (NIV). But whoever refuses discipline and lives an unruly, disorderly, and reprobate life is a ticking time bomb ready to explode, shattering the lives of those close enough to be impacted by the blast.

Tradition does not save you. Good works will not open the doors of Heaven for you. Singing "Amazing Grace" on Easter morning does not make you a disciple of Jesus.

It's not what you believe. It's what you obey. Doing what God has asked you to do is what makes you a disciple.

Jesus demanded discipline. His followers were called disciples. If you're not disciplined, you're not in the fold. I want you to understand that. *"To the Jews who had believed him, Jesus said, 'If you hold to my teaching, you are really my disciples'"* (John 8:31, NIV). The measure of a true disciple is a man or woman who holds fast to the teachings of Jesus.

> It's not what you believe. It's what you obey. Doing what God has asked you to do is what makes you a disciple.

Willpower and Human Nature

Human nature is predisposed to selfishness from a young age. A word common to every toddler the world over is, "Mine!" Toddlers know how to say "mine," but disciples of Jesus must learn to say, "Thy will be done." If we are to grow as followers of Jesus, we must embrace discipline.

The apostle Paul was a disciple and a disciplined Christian. He governed his body saying, *"I discipline my body and keep it under control, lest after preaching to others I myself should be disqualified"* (1 Corinthians 9:27, ESV). Discipline of the body leads to discipline in other areas in our lives.

Paul lived a disciplined life. He disciplined himself to scorn, saying that he had become a fool for Christ's sake (1 Corinthians 4:10). He disciplined himself to suffering, saying, *"We are hard-pressed on every side, yet not crushed; we are perplexed, but not in despair; persecuted, but not forsaken; struck down, but not destroyed"* (2 Corinthians 4:8–9, NKJV). Paul never stopped advancing the Gospel because he had decided to keep going no matter what.

In the end, he disciplined himself to the knowledge that he would die for Christ's sake. *"For I am already being poured out as a drink offering, and the time of my departure is at hand. I have fought the good fight, I have finished the race, I have kept the faith"* (2 Timothy 4:6–7, NKJV). Paul was ready to face death because he had given his life to do the will of the Master.

You can live a disciplined life as well. You can be a Holy Spirit-anointed, dedicated, in-season, and out-of-season Christian. You can deny yourself and fast and pray. You can go to church even if it rains. You can study the Word of God. If you do, you'll find that it's still alive, it's still the bread of life, it's still living water, and it's still the compass for your soul.

You have what it takes to become a disciplined follower of Jesus Christ. You don't have to be controlled by the world, the flesh, and the devil. You don't have to be controlled by emotions or feelings that come and go and drag you by the nose down the road of life. That does not fit you. You do not have to be tossed to and fro on the waves of life because you are a blood-bought, redeemed child of God.

The first step toward living the disciplined life of a believer is to fully commit yourself to absolute reliance on Jesus Christ as Savior, Lord, and King over your life. It is deciding that you will seek God above all else. It is rejecting the trappings, cares, and glitter of life and instead fixing your eyes on God Most High. Jesus demands full devotion. The call to follow Christ encompasses all.

You cannot dabble in the affairs of the world and pledge allegiance to Jesus as Lord of your life.

Following yourself won't get you anywhere, but following Jesus will lead you to life. In the world we will have trial, tribulation, and trouble, but Jesus said, *"He who endures to the end shall be saved"* (Matthew 24:13, NKJV). To endure to the end means that no matter what the world may throw at you, and no matter what may come — as for you — you are committed, dedicated, and faithful to follow Jesus Christ forevermore.

> The first step toward living the disciplined life of a believer is to fully commit yourself to absolute reliance on Jesus Christ as Savior, Lord, and King over your life.

When There
Is No God

Here is important news. We are running our final lap before the rapture of the church. If there was ever a time for you to give it everything you have and finish strong, it's right now. The goal for you is to serve the Lord and complete the work God has called you to do.

When there is no God, man comes up with philosophies to frame an understanding of life. One is called self-negation. This viewpoint states that man's instincts are so fierce that we must find a way to destroy them. Religions of the world will teach the same, and I've heard a lot of preachers get very close to that. The way it works is that if you have no desire, you're never upset. If you expect nothing, you'll never be disappointed. But it also means you live a shell of a life.

But the Bible says, *"Take delight in the LORD and he will give you the desires of your heart"* (Psalm 37:4, NIV). If God says that He will give us the desires of our heart, and world religions are saying to kill all our desires to reach Heaven, there's a major conflict of thought. One says to reduce your desires to zero and you'll never be disappointed. On the other hand, the Bible says that when we delight in the Lord, He gives us our heart's desire. I believe God is right since He's the Creator of Heaven and earth.

Cowboys break the will of horses to tame them so they can ride them. But they do not break the spirit of the horse. If they do that, the horse is worthless. Similarly, if you break the human spirit, there is no passion for life, no purpose, no dream, and no vision. What's the solution? It is neither to let man's passion run free with no restraint nor to deny the desires that make you a person, but rather to follow the blueprint of the Bible — to seek first the Kingdom of God, to harness passions and desires in a godly way, and then experience the joy of reaching your divine destiny.

When there is no God, life unravels at the seams. Without God, there is no Creator of the world, there is no reason to adhere to law and order, and there is no real purpose for life. Without God, the fabric of reality can be redefined because God is out of the picture. Without God, man becomes his own chief end. And when man is his own god, chaos and narcissism reign free. We are seeing that in our world today.

So, what happens? Without God, many people try to control their lives with worship of their own will. But "will worship" is idolatry. Will worship says, "I am the master of my faith. I am the captain of my soul." But if you say that, you're not following God; you're following yourself, and you are making yourself and your own will an idol.

Your individual willpower is not strong enough to conquer the power of sin. I've heard many men boast of their willpower, saying, "I have the will of steel."

But if you say that, your trust is in your flesh and not in God. You're worshiping what you can do for you, not what Christ has already done for you. And there's a world of difference between those two.

But there is a God in Heaven and He has a good plan for your life. When you submit your will to Him, your life will come into order. If you're wondering what God's will is for you, 1 Thessalonians 4:3 says, *"This is the will of God, your sanctification"* (ESV). God's will for you is to submit your will to Him, to become more like Jesus, and in doing so, find true joy in His plan for you.

> There is a God in Heaven and He has a good plan for your life. When you submit your will to Him, your life will come into order.

Harness Your
Passion

The Bible holds a formula you can follow to harness the wild horses of your passions. It is a time-tested and proven method straight from the Word of God, and it will not fail you. It is the Biblical path of pursuing a lifestyle of discipline as you grow in your walk with God.

Discipline is an exercise of your free will. The same instincts that made Napoleon great were in the apostle Paul as well. The difference between the two is that Paul's instincts were harnessed by the Holy Spirit, while Napoleon's never were. Napoleon could conquer the world, but he could never conquer himself, though indeed he tried.

The answer to harnessing the wild horses of the body, soul, and will is to submit them wholly to the Lordship of Jesus Christ. When you do, then you can put them to work, ride them, and rejoice in their strength. Proverbs 18:16 says, *"A man's gift makes room for him and brings him before the great"* (ESV). When you live a disciplined life and the rule of your spirit is in submission to God, you will find the door is open for you to let the strengths and gifts God has given you carry you to staggering heights of accomplishment.

Discipline is key to achievement. Godly ambition can be harnessed when it is disciplined. Look at the men Jesus chose to be His disciples. Would you have chosen Matthew? He was a tax collector. In those days, tax collectors were despised because of how crooked they were. But when Jesus looked at Matthew and said, *"Follow me"* (Matthew 9:9, ESV), he gave up his lucrative profession, followed Jesus, and never looked back.

The disciples weren't trembly-lipped wildflowers, looking for someone to identify with. They were ambitious men who wanted to get ahead in the world, and they even wanted to get ahead of each other. The last week Jesus was alive, James and John went to Him and said, *"Grant us that we may sit, one on Your right hand and the other on Your left, in Your glory"* (Mark 10:37, NKJV). Forget these other 10, we want to be Mr. Big and Mr. Semi-Big!

But Jesus didn't rebuke them for their request to hold places of honor. He harnessed that ambition and called the disciples together and said, *"Whoever of you desires to be first shall be slave of all. For even the Son of Man did not come to be served, but to serve, and to give His life a ransom for many"* (vv. 44–45).

Again, in the upper room, He demonstrated what it meant to be great in God's Kingdom. Mere hours before He would be betrayed, He put a towel on His arm and knelt and washed the disciples' feet saying, *"The greatest among you will be your servant"* (Matthew 23:11, NIV). What was He doing? He was showing the portrait of absolute power in total control.

Christ is our example (1 Peter 2:21). He had all power in Heaven and on earth, and yet He demonstrated discipline and control even upon the Cross. When you harness your wild horse emotions, your habits, your fears, and your frustrations, you will produce fruit that lasts. Seek to become servant of all, and in doing so, you will find what it means to become great in Heaven's eyes.

> The answer to harnessing the wild horses of the body, soul, and will is to submit them wholly to the Lordship of Jesus Christ.

Heavyweights

Saul of Tarsus had a raging temper. He was a born fighter. He was Type A — turbo-driven, hard-headed, and aggressive — and loved to argue with anyone about anything. To resist him only encouraged him. But God saw Saul and said, "I want him. I don't want some wildflower who never opens his mouth. I want that one right there." On the Damascus road, God knocked him off his horse. All Saul could say was, *"Who are you, Lord?"* (Acts 9:5, ESV). He encountered Christ and turned his life around. Immediately he began proclaiming Jesus in the synagogues saying, *"He is the Son of God"* (v. 20). By harnessing who Paul was, God turned him loose, and he shook the Roman Empire to its knees by the anointing of the Holy Spirit.

God is not looking for wildflowers who will bow before the prince of darkness. He's not looking for cautious believers who tremble before every roaring lion. He's looking for strong, aggressive, wild horses to harness, who will run their race with excellence, who will fight the good fight of faith, who will endure hardness, and who will resist the devil and watch him flee.

In December 1971, on a Wednesday night, I was teaching my congregation about the Biblical position on demonology. A gunman came into the building and roared like a lion. He walked up the aisle, cursing like a sailor, pointed his gun at me, and said, "I've come to kill you in front of this congregation to demonstrate that Satan has more power than Jesus Christ." I held up my Bible and said, "This is the Word of God. It says no weapon formed against me shall prosper." He said, "I have a gun." I said, "I have the Word of God." He wanted me to beg for my life, but I said, "I am in authority here. Not you." He shot six shots from eight feet away and took off. All six missed me, three to the left and three to the right.[xvi] The power of God is real, and you need to know that greater is He who is in you than he who is in the world (1 John 4:4).

God has called the church to be a victorious army. To overcome the enemy by the blood of the Lamb and the word of our testimony. Let God arise, and may His enemies be scattered! Put your hand to the plow for whatever work the Lord has called you to do. Don't look back but keep taking the victory and advancing the Gospel in Christ's name.

To do any great work will take self-control, discipline, and the power of faith. But without self-control, you'll lose it all. Look at the boneyard of human history: men and women who had everything but lost it because they didn't have self-control.

Adam and Eve lived in paradise, but the price of the forbidden fruit destroyed it all. If the citizens of Sodom and Gomorrah could rise from the ashes of destruction, they would tell you, *"Fear God, and keep his commandments"* (Ecclesiastes 12:13, KJV). If Samson could testify today, he would tell you that his eyes were gouged out and he was made to grind grain like a slave because he could not walk away from the lust of the flesh.

By the power of the Holy Spirit, you can overcome the enemy. You are not here on this earth simply to sail into the "sweet by-and by." You have a call of God on your life. You are here to push back the darkness, rescue souls from Hell, and make famous the name of Jesus throughout the earth. And by the grace of God, you will do so, and "even greater works than these" (John 14:12).

> God has called the church to be a victorious army. To overcome the enemy by the blood of the Lamb and the word of our testimony.

Discipline vs. Punishment

Do you understand the difference between discipline and punishment? A disciplined person can achieve much because they have rule over their bodies, minds, and emotions. A disciplined person will attain to heights that an undisciplined person never will. Two of the most well-known ministers in church history who lived disciplined lives were John and Charles Wesley. Their attention to religious practice was so organized, and their lives so tuned to methodical discipline, that their following grew and would eventually establish both the Wesleyan and Methodist churches.[xvii] The discipline of two brothers sparked far-reaching moves of God.

Punishment is something different entirely. Punishment is correction for doing wrong. The level of punishment may fit the crime, as in the case of a felon sent to prison for life for some heinous crime. But punishment is usually an outward effect appropriated upon another person. Discipline, however, is a work that one gives themselves to for the purpose of advancement. It is instruction on how to do something to change your destiny.

Do you have discipline? You better get it, because if you don't, you'll never achieve your dream. You'll never achieve the destiny God has for you if you live a slothful, lazy life. Proverbs 12:24 says, *"The hand of the diligent will rule, while the slothful will be put to forced labor"* (ESV). You'll never become what God designed for you to become from the beginning unless you are disciplined, diligent, and hard-working.

In spiritual matters, if you refuse discipline, you're not in the family of God. Hebrews 12:7–8 says, *"It is for discipline that you have to endure. God is treating you as sons. For what son is there whom his father does not discipline? If you are left without discipline, in which all have participated, then you are illegitimate children and not sons"* (ESV). If you have a King James Version, get ready for a shock because the King James Version uses a much stronger word than "illegitimate" in verse eight.

Discipline will bring success in any area of life. When you go to college, there's an academic discipline you must conquer. And if you don't pick it up quickly, you'll be failing out. When you get married, there's the discipline of marriage and upholding your vows. When you join the church, there's a spiritual discipline to live by as you grow in sanctification (Galatians 5:16–24).

In the Marine Corps, new recruits are sent to boot camp to begin training for military life. They get up in the middle of the night, their drill instructor becomes the new best friend they wish they never had, and they are transformed into lean, mean, fighting machines.

Why? So when they enter the throes of combat, they stand their ground. On April 22nd, 2008, in Ramadi, the discipline of two marines who had been "forged in the same crucible of Marine training" passed the test. They were on guard duty at 7:30 a.m. when a truck carrying 2,000 pounds of explosives barreled down on the barracks they were guarding. For six seconds, they stood their ground, emptying their magazines at the truck. They neutralized the threat, but in the process, they lost their own lives.[xviii] That day, the discipline of two Marines saved the lives of 150 American and Iraqi allied lives.

When you get saved, Jesus takes you to boot camp. This is not punishment, this is discipline. And He begins to transform you into a man or woman who can push back the enemy and do the work of the Lord upon the earth. You are here for a reason, and it is to do great things for the Kingdom of God!

> Discipline will bring success in any area of life.

Our Kingdom Mission

God has an incredibly good plan for your life. He has a plan for your life that will bring you joy and increase the work of the Gospel across the earth. But to lay hold of that plan, you will have to work hard, and you will have to live a disciplined, God-focused life.

God's plan for you is attainable. A key step is immersing yourself in the study of God's Word. Jesus said, *"If you abide in My word, you are My disciples indeed"* (John 8:31, NKJV). To abide in the Word of God, you must read the Word, study the Word, and meditate on the Word. It must become what your heart is full of, so that when life squeezes you, the Word of God is what comes out.

The level you attain in achieving God's plan for your life is directly correlated to how submitted you are to the Lordship of Jesus. In Luke 6:46, Jesus said, *"Why do you call me 'Lord, Lord,' and not do what I tell you?"* (ESV). It will never be enough to know of Jesus, to be familiar with Jesus, or even to call Jesus "Lord." Obedience of our hearts must follow the words we say.

Obedience will propel you in your walk with God. Obedience is a bigger deal in the Kingdom of God than you may realize because it is better than sacrifice (1 Samuel 15:22). Philippians 2 tells us that Jesus Himself was obedient. He took on the nature of a servant, was made in human likeness, and humbled Himself by becoming obedient to death — even death on a cross (Philippians 2:8).

The Cross will cost you everything. One day, a rich young ruler came up to Jesus and said, *"What shall I do so that I may inherit eternal life?"* (Mark 10:17, NASB). He believed that Jesus was the Messiah. Jesus said, *"Go and sell all you possess and give to the poor, and you will have treasure in heaven; and come, follow Me"* (v. 21). Jesus knew he had a problem with material things. But the rich young ruler was more concerned with himself than with the mission of God. He could not put away his wealth to follow Christ.

In the darkest moments of Jesus' life, He was kneeling in the garden of Gethsemane, praying. He said, *"My Father, if it is possible, may this cup be taken from me. Yet not as I will, but as you will"* (Matthew 26:39, NIV). With the Cross before Him, blood dripping from His brow, and the sins of the world to atone for, He prayed. Nevertheless, He was resolved to obedience and said, *"Yet not as I will, but as you will."* He went to the Cross and became the propitiation of men.

Judas sold Him for 30 pieces of silver. Peter denied Him. The Pretorian Guard scourged Him with a cat-o'-nine-tails. Roman hands took the nails and drove them through His hands and feet. At any second, He could have called 10,000 angels. But what did Jesus do? He said, *"Father, forgive them, for they do not know what they do"* (Luke 23:34, NKJV). Through obedience and discipline, Jesus conquered all.

What has the Lord called you to do? What has He put on your heart? What is it that you think about year after year? You can live a disciplined Christian life in obedience to the Word of God. In Christ, you can fulfill God's purposes and plans for you. By the anointing of the Holy Spirit, you can take control of your life, live holy and separated from the world, and complete the destiny the Lord has set before you.

> The level you attain in achieving God's plan for your life is directly correlated to how submitted you are to the Lordship of Jesus.

Endnotes

I.   https://www.brainyquote.com/quotes/edmund_burke_377528

II.   https://www.govinfo.gov/content/pkg/USCODE-2010-title10/
        html/USCODE-2010-title10-subtitleA-partII-chap31-sec502.htm

III.   https://www.history.com/topics/
        womens-history/florence-nightingale-1

IV.   https://www.poetryfoundation.org/poems/44172/absalom-and-achitophel

V.   https://www.ncbi.nlm.nih.gov/pmc/articles/PMC6609137/

VI.   https://www.britannica.com/science/penicillin

VII.   https://hymnary.org/
        text/i_hear_the_savior_say_thy_strength_indee

VIII.   https://hymnary.org/text/i_come_to_the_garden_alone

IX.   https://www.christianity.com/wikiprayerwhat-
        is-the-serenity-prayer-is-it-biblical.html

X.   https://www.britannica.com/topic/Titanic

XI.   https://www.christianity.com/church/church-history/
        timeline/1701-1800/john-newton-discovered-amazing-grace-11630253.html

XII.   https://sourcebooks.fordham.edu/mod/nietzsche-madman.asp

XIII.   Dietrich Bonhoeffer, *The Cost of Discipleship*
        (New York: Touchstone, 1959), 58

XIV.   https://www.irishcentral.com/roots/
        st-patricks-breastplate-prayer-irelands-patron-saint

XV.   https://www.army.mil/article/183328/
        pfc_desmond_doss_the_unlikely_hero_behind_hacksaw_ridge

XVI.   John Hagee: Angelic Protection (James Robison / LIFEToday)
        https://www.youtube.com/watch?v=K7Vz8KseTxw

XVII.   https://www.britannica.com/biography/Charles-Wesley

XVIII. https://www.businessinsider.com/john-kellys-speech-truck-bomb-2017-4

"Teacher, which is the great commandment in the law?" Jesus said to him,

"'You shall love the LORD your God with all your heart, with all your soul, and with all your mind.'

This is the first and great commandment. And the second is like it: 'You shall love your neighbor as yourself.' On these two commandments hang all the Law and the Prophets."

MATTHEW 22:36–40 (NKJV)

About the Author

John Hagee is the founder and senior pastor of Cornerstone Church in San Antonio, Texas, a nondenominational evangelical church with more than 22,000 active members. He is the author of more than forty books, including several *New York Times* Bestsellers, his latest being *Earth's Last Empire: The Final Game of Thrones*. Pastor Hagee is the founder and chairman of Christians United for Israel (CUFI), with over 11 million followers. Hagee Ministries television and radio outreach spans America and the nations of the world.

To learn more about Pastor John Hagee, visit:

Hagee Ministries:
jhm.org

Facebook
HageeMinistries

Twitter
PastorJohnHagee
HageeMinistries

Instagram
PastorJohnHagee
HageeMinistries

Wild HORSES

All of us have emotions that must be corralled if we are
to achieve our destiny in life. One of the most difficult
aspects of a Christian's life is learning how to control our
emotions. Unbridled emotions are a door for Satan to attack
your health, mind, relationships, and life. In this devotional,
Pastor Hagee gives clear, Biblical points on how you can
overcome the torrent of emotions that buffet against your
soul and harness them to further the Kingdom of God.

ISBN 978-1-951701-43-7

9 781951 701437